CHALLENGE THE NORM AND
MAKE GREAT MISTAKES!

Young Professional's

GUIDE TO

SUCCESS

Young Professional's

GUIDE TO

SUCCESS

———

RYAN KOHNEN

EMERALD
BOOK CO.

Published by Emerald Book Company
Austin, TX
www.emeraldbookcompany.com

Distributed by Emerald Book Company

For ordering information or special discounts for bulk purchases, please contact Emerald Book Company at PO Box 91869, Austin, TX 78709, 512.891.6100.

Design and composition by DESIGNS for Every Occasion
Cover design by Uppercase Design Group

Publisher's Cataloging-in-Publication Data

Kohnen, Ryan, 1980-
   Young professional's guide to success / [written and compiled by] Ryan Kohnen.
   -- 1st ed.

   p. : ill. ; cm.

   ISBN: 978-1-934572-25-2

1. Success in business. 2. Success--Psychological aspects. 3. Career development. I. Title.

HF5386 .K64 2009
650.1   2009928588

Part of the Tree Neutral™ program, which offsets the number of trees consumed in the production and printing of this book by taking proactive steps, such as planting trees in direct proportion to the number of trees used: www.treeneutral.com

TreeNeutral

Printed in the United States of America on acid-free paper

09 10 11 12 13 14   10 9 8 7 6 5 4 3 2 1

First Edition

DEDICATIONS

TO MY WIFE, LACEY. You keep me grounded, honest, and humble, but still allow me to pursue my dreams—however crazy and big they are. Thanks for smiling, supporting, and nodding at every one of my ideas to change the world! Randall Fox was dead-on (p. 186).

TO MY MOM AND DAD. Thank you for giving me everything I need so I can accomplish anything that I want. You both are great examples of working hard and taking advantage of every opportunity presented to you.

Finally, a special thank you to all of the executives and leaders that contributed to this book. I now consider all of you "mini-mentors." Your wisdom and experiences you shared in this book helped me achieve one of my dreams, and I hope it can help other young professionals achieve theirs.

CONTENTS

GENERATION A.D.D.
Who this book is for, why it was written, and how to use it as a reference

1

This section was originally going to be labeled "Introduction"—but chances are, if you're like me, you always skip the introduction and go straight to Chapter One.

Like myself, you are a young professional, or about to become one, and your days are filled with television, Internet, satellite radio, video games (unimaginative ones, not like the eight-bit Nintendo we grew up with), mobile phones, CrackBerrys, and other distractions that have caused an entire age bracket to earn the moniker: "Generation A.D.D." (attention deficit disorder). I'm sure I am not the only one who sits on his living room couch with his laptop, watching television while surfing the Web using a wireless Internet connection (multiple windows open, of course), and his trusty BlackBerry within reach on the coffee table. Of course, I also have my remote control handy, to avoid commercials while switching back and forth among the two hundred channels.

BLOG ME:
ypsuccess.com
Share your favorite books.

We want information, and we want it now.

In searching for this information, my library of business, leadership, and entrepreneurship books has grown exponentially. It is now approaching two hundred volumes, and yet out of those, I believe I have read every word in only ten:

- *Winning*, Jack Welch
- *Good to Great*, Jim Collins
- *Your Marketing Sucks*, Mark Stevens
- *Made to Stick*, Chip Heath and Dan Heath
- *The Knack*, Norm Brodsky and Bo Burlingham
- *No More Mondays*, Dan Miller

- *Talent Is Overrated*, Geoff Colvin
- *The Tipping Point*, Malcolm Gladwell
- *The 17 Indisputable Laws of Teamwork*, John C. Maxwell
- *The Millionaire Next Door*, Thomas J. Stanley and William D. Danko

The most frustrating part of reading most business books is that they are nearly impossible to reference at a later time, when you actually need that information. Searching for that one essential quote or concept is like searching for a needle in a haystack.

This book dodges that trend. Because I suffer along with the rest of Generation A.D.D., I have too many stimuli in my house to read without distraction. I wanted to put together and offer exactly what I would look for in a book: one that is short and to the point, and that provides me with practical value. You can go directly to topics of interest, read for fifteen minutes and pick up a lesson or two, and then reference them easily at a later time. This is not a book that has only one theme. It includes a variety of topics, pieces of advice, and stories concerning all facets of a young career and the personal life of a young professional.

In 2003, I founded the organization Young Execs in San Antonio, Texas. It was created for a variety of reasons, but none was as important as getting business and community leaders to interact with young professionals. Those leaders shared their stories of success and failure, which will prove invaluable to the next generation of leaders. I have used that model of learning for this book. You will find quotes and stories from CEOs and industry leaders, from small business owners and young business leaders. The other purposes for founding Young Execs were building relationships and getting involved in the community—two aspects that will be touched upon throughout this book. Although the San

Antonio chapter is no longer around, I am proud to say that Young Execs of Austin is alive and well.

Through my involvement with Young Execs and my work with other young professional organizations, I have had the opportunity to collaborate and talk with thousands of young professionals in the past few years, and with business owners and managers who employ young professionals. These people are the experts—the young professionals and executives who have made mistakes or enjoyed success. I have simply taken their information and advice and put it in a format for easy reading.

I love learning and reading about the business world. But so many books about business are nothing more than an entertaining read, with little valuable information that could have a significant impact on one's career. There are a few books that I keep close by my side, however, both as reminders of the important messages they present and as a reference for future discussions. I am judging the success of this book much as I judge the books that I read: if I can walk away with a few really good pieces of advice or some concepts that can make a difference in my life, it was worth it. I hope you will be able to say the same.

I would love to hear about what items of significance influenced you or any comments you may wish to share. **Please e-mail me. I will personally respond to each of you—your feedback is my reward for the time and effort that I have spent on this project.** However, please keep them short, because I'll be reading them on my couch while watching television and surfing the Internet.

Your fellow young professional,
Ryan Kohnen
ryan@ryankohnen.com

GLOSSARY OF SYMBOLS

 SPEECH BUBBLE: Invitation to share thoughts with the author via e-mail, blog, or twitter.

 PULL QUOTE: Points of interest.

 CAREER KILLER: Advice on what not to do during your career.

 TIDBITS: Words to live by.

 YIELD: Suggested reading or websites to visit.

ARE YOU PREPARED FOR SUCCESS?
Preparing for a successful career begins early.

2

A few years ago, a business mentor of mine came to me with one of the best questions I have ever been asked: "Are you prepared for success?" At the time, I was fully convinced that I was ready for success and all that came with it. This gentleman sat down with me and we mapped out my past experiences, my accomplishments, my strengths and weaknesses, and where I wanted to be in five years, ten years, and beyond. The more I began to look at where I was and where I wanted to be, the more I realized that I was not ready to get there.

As a college sophomore in 1999, I did what a lot of entrepreneurial college students did at that time: I started my own Web business. In a bedroom of my parents' house, I started a website design company (without any experience in Web design—that's a book in itself!), and within six months I began to see tremendous growth and opportunity. In December 1999, I decided that the opportunity to grow the business was more important than spending time in the classroom working on my degree. Although my business saw great success in the three years that I owned it, when all was said and done, no one handed me a degree for the experience and knowledge that I gained.

> "*Get a college degree, and complete it within four years of graduating from high school.*"

My first major piece of advice: get a college degree, and complete it within four years of graduating from high school.

I finally went back to school at age twenty-four to complete my education, and although I don't regret any of the choices I made in my career path, I would surely advise against following a similar path. Finish college first, and then take a look at all the wonderful business opportunities that are out there.

When I first went back to school I had a great conversation with a young man about earning a college degree. He was thirty-two years old, had never received one, and was enjoying a successful sales career. After mentioning that I was back in school after a four-year break, he looked at me, smiling, and said, "That's great. I really would like to get my degree. I have learned that a degree won't open many doors for you, but not having one sure shuts a lot of them."

If you already have your college degree or will soon earn it, you should be congratulated for your accomplishment! A word of warning: Do not expect that a degree entitles you to a well-paying job or a great career. You can be assured that without the degree, however, your options will be limited.

> "*A degree won't open many doors for you, but not having one sure shuts a lot of them.*"

With his question about being prepared for success, the business mentor's goal was to find out whether I was ready to be as successful as I could be. When it came to my five-year goals, everything appeared to be in order. I had quite a bit of experience in sales and marketing, public speaking, and public relations, and so I determined that I was ready for success. He then asked me what some of my long-term goals in my career were. I told him I wanted to be a CEO or founder of a major company.

Being a founder of a company does not require a college degree, it's true. But when I began reading the biographies of successful CEOs of major companies, I learned that having an undergraduate degree is a given, and a graduate degree is almost expected if one is to reach CEO status in a major corporation. It was obvious at this point that in fact I was not truly ready for success.

As the thirty-two-year-old without a degree said, the degree will not open doors for you automatically—that is your job. But it sure helps you to get started on your path to success. Setting yourself up for a successful career begins much earlier than when you start your first full-time job. Achieving success may require more preparation than you might expect.

Look at the people who have the jobs that you might like to have in the future. What type of education or experiences do they have that you don't? What did they do early in their career that helped set them up for success? Even if you have a degree already, you can learn from this exercise: Where would you like to be in five, ten, or twenty years? What sort of education or experience will be required for you to get there?

Now you have action items. Now you have some tools and items that you can work on in the short term to benefit your long-term plans.

* * * * * * * * * *

Small business owners form a unique bond and share the pains and joys of being self-employed. I had a great group of friends that came out of my small business owners' circle. There was an ongoing conversation about how well our employees were doing and how we could grow and flourish. This group tended to hire younger employees recently out of college. Why? Because you could always find a recent college graduate who would be an energetic employee willing to work for less money.

So what exactly did we all look for during the hiring process? Believe it or not, most of us never even looked at GPA. One of my colleagues constantly complained, "What did these kids do in college? Just study all day?" He wasn't downplaying the importance of studying, but he felt that a student with a 4.0 grade point average who was "only a student" wasn't as valuable as a student with a 3.0 GPA that held a part-time job, volunteered at a local charity, and had strong communication skills. Our entire group agreed with that concept.

This doesn't mean that your GPA is not important; if your experience and extracurricular activities match up with another candidate, your GPA may put you over the top. The point is that your future employers will often focus on your extracurricular activities to get an idea of who you really are. So get involved in school organizations, or get a part-time job or an internship.

Try not to be tempted to take the $10- or $12-an-hour job somewhere you can't see yourself working after you graduate, just because it pays well. A job that may pad your current pocketbook may do little for your future pocketbook and career. Try to work or intern (yes, that may mean no pay) somewhere you might see yourself working after college. Not only will you gain valuable experience in a field that you enjoy, but you may find yourself working there full-time once you graduate.

> "*Do not under-estimate the value of volunteering at nonprofit organizations*"

If you didn't have a part-time job or an internship in college and you are currently looking for a job, volunteer your time at a nonprofit during your job search. Try to use the skills that you have learned in college to benefit the nonprofit. If you have an accounting degree, try to find a nonprofit organization in need of some bookkeeping assistance. This will give you instant experience in your field and will allow you to start building a portfolio of work. This concept will be stressed later in the book: do not underestimate the value of volunteering at nonprofit organizations! This type of work will strengthen your self-worth and feelings of goodwill, and it is also an opportunity to make excellent business contacts.

Throughout this book you will see stories in large, boldface boxes. Some give insightful information and guidance about how to succeed as you're starting your career—and some are what I call Career Killers. These are the tales of established leaders—pieces of advice for young professionals about particular items that can ruin a career. As our discussion moves from college days to the years beyond, the first Career Killer—from Jack Prim, president and CEO of Jack Henry & Associates—is extremely appropriate.

Jack Prim

Chief Executive Officer

JACK HENRY & ASSOCIATES

One thing that comes to mind is to be very careful with alcohol in a company setting. This is good advice for anyone. I have seen forty-year-olds commit corporate suicide in this environment. I can especially see how a young professional or someone right out of college might think, "Open bar? Sweet! Toga, toga!"

Many years ago as a national sales manager, I hired a sales rep into the organization. We were at a company retreat at Pinehurst, where we were kicking off the start of a new sales year. Everyone in the company who had a sales role was there, along with almost all of the company's senior management team.

The individual whom I had hired drank all the way to Pinehurst and pretty steadily after his arrival and through dinner. He became absolutely obnoxious and alienated pretty much everybody he came in contact with. The president of the company pulled me aside and said, "As far as I'm concerned, you can fire that idiot and send him home tonight." This guy probably could not have found his car, let alone his way home. I ended up saving his job, but there was pretty much no opportunity for him ever to advance in the company after that.

This is something you can only fully appreciate if you are the only sober person at a party. Try it sometime; it can actually be quite amusing.

About once a year, usually right before a marathon, I'll stop drinking for about ninety days to lose any unnecessary weight so I don't have to haul it twenty-six miles. It is very entertaining to watch people over the course of an evening as the drinks keep flowing. Some people can't keep their clothes on. Others get loud or foul-mouthed, and have no idea they are doing it. Sometimes people want to make long, passionate speeches, which frequently also incorporate the loud and foul-mouthed characteristics.

My advice in a professional setting is to assume somebody is always watching. Drink club soda. But if you have to drink alcohol, limit yourself to two drinks, and take your time with them. And if you see anyone coming toward you with a shot or a bottle of tequila, turn and run as fast as you can in the other direction.

I couldn't have put it more plainly myself.

ENTITLEMENT DISORDER

*You've graduated from college—does this mean
that you deserve a corner office?*

3

In 2003 a good friend of mine, Mark Desjardins, gave a talk called
"Entitlement Disorder" at one of our Young Execs lunches. I had
never heard the term at the time, nor did I fully understand it, but
I've since realized the role it plays in people's lives.

Many of us have to fight Entitlement Disorder. I will admit
that with my business experience and a college degree, I sometimes have felt a bit "entitled" to a well-paying job, or as if certain
work was "beneath me." This probably includes those jobs that
most people consider unsuitable for a college graduate: anything
that involves getting their hands dirty.

Much of the problem is caused by our fascination with celeb-
rities and the life we see on reality television shows. As some of us
live vicariously through the characters in these reality shows, it is
easy to believe that the waterfront home, an unlimited entertainment allowance, and designer clothes are something we deserve
and should have. We want it, and we want it now. We also, of
course, want to do the minimum amount of work required to pay
for all of this. It is no mystery why young professionals are drown-
ing in debt. We are living beyond our means, because most of us
feel we are entitled to have everything. (Read more on debt and
financial obligations in the next chapter, "Establishing Values.")

James Ellis, dean of the Marshall School of Business at the
University of Southern California, offers one of my favorite examples of not giving in to Entitlement Disorder. Just two months after
Dean Ellis received his master's degree in business administration
from Harvard University, he was sitting on the concrete floor of
a distribution center, sorting purses according to color. What a

visual! Can you imagine someone who had just completed one of the most prestigious graduate programs in the world doing something that most would assume is reserved for minimum-wage workers? I tell this story often, because even for those of us who feel we do not suffer from Entitlement Disorder, that story really hits home. It did for me. If I had been asked to do what Dean Ellis did, I would have probably scoffed in the face of the requester! And I don't even have an MBA from Harvard.

James G. Ellis

Dean of the Marshall School of Business
UNIVERSITY OF SOUTHERN CALIFORNIA

If I were to encapsulate what worked best for me in the early days of my career, I would say it was the ability to say "yes" every time I was asked by my bosses to do something.

I was a trainee in the retailing world of large department stores, and was asked to do some things that many of us might shy away from for one reason or another, such as:

Just say YES.

- Drive a forklift to unload boxcars in 100-degree heat—while being forced to keep my tie on because I was a trainee!
- Transfer from the main office to a store on November 1, knowing full well I would be going from forty hours a week to one hundred hours a week for the next eight weeks.
- Go to the offices of senior managers to tell them that they were not operating within policy in distribution of their merchandise, and that they needed to get their people to conform.

- Stay late—and I mean late.
- Come in early—and I mean early. Sometimes this even meant coming in on Saturday or Sunday to finish a project.
- Fly to Europe for a meeting tomorrow morning (talk about last-minute!), and fly back the next day.
- Go to dinner with a visiting company president from New York because no one else wanted to play "tour guide."
- Travel with another buyer to Mongolia, just because the company did not want him going there by himself.

Every time I did one of these tasks, it was recognized that I was willing to take on more than just what my job description said, and that I would go the extra mile for the company.

The rewards that came from just saying "yes" were huge. I met people I would not have ordinarily met, and I remain friends with them today; I saw parts of the world I would never have otherwise seen, and became comfortable in any environment; I experienced parts of the business that I would not have otherwise understood well.

Just say "yes" when asked, and if you have the chance, even volunteer before they ask you. The benefits are significant, and although they may not come for years, you will recognize them when they do.

If there is an MBA candidate doing the exact opposite of Dr. Ellis, it would be the one witnessed by Dr. Linda Livingstone, dean of the Graziadio School of Business and Management at Pepperdine University.

Linda A. Livingstone, PhD

Dean of the Graziadio School of Business and Management

PEPPERDINE UNIVERSITY

I was serving as associate dean of graduate programs for a business school. We had planned an event with a speaker and had invited all the MBA students to attend.

Do whatever is needed to get the job done.

As I arrived early the morning of the event and went to check on the room setup, I realized that some changes needed to be made in order to best accommodate the speaker and the attendees. Given the time frame, I began to rearrange the room with the help of other faculty and students who had arrived early.

Among those who had arrived early were two married students who both attended the MBA program. The husband jumped in along with other students and began moving chairs around. A few minutes later, I noticed his wife approach him—they were close enough to me that I could overhear the conversation. She proceeded to tell him that he needed to quit moving chairs, as that was not something he should be doing—implying that it was beneath him to do that type of work.

Needless to say, I was shocked that one of our students would have this attitude, particularly as all the others—faculty, staff, administration, and other students alike—were pitching in to help. My career advice from this: it is important to be willing to do whatever work is needed to get the job done, particularly early in one's career. This willingness to work sets a great example, is noticed by others, and is the right thing to do.

A willingness to work and an appropriately humble nature are major antidotes to Entitlement Disorder—one that the young professional in the next example could have benefited from.

Todd Klingel

President & CEO

MINNEAPOLIS REGIONAL CHAMBER OF COMMERCE

Much has been written about what steps the baby boomer generation must take to address the needs of Generation Xers and Millennials. I have not seen as much discourse on how young professionals should prepare in return.

It would be wise for those who seek to advance in work and in the world today to spend some time appreciating how their supervisors view the process. There is no question that enlightened employers seeking top new talent will make every effort to understand and accommodate young professionals. However, the aspiring worker should not expect a wholesale change in how an organization operates.

Here is an example: we parted ways with one young person in our employ, because when we informed the employee that we were going to have him work out of a nearby office a few days a week, the response was, "How could you make this decision without consulting me?"

This advice is important no matter what business you're in. Remember: passion, ambition, and humility—the opposite of a sense of entitlement—translate to career success in any industry.

Mark Desjardins, PhD
Head of School
HOLLAND HALL

Mark recommends *How to Become CEO,* by Jeffrey J. Fox

During your first few years on the job, never say no. Volunteer for everything, and be totally committed to the company. The idea is to expose yourself to every facet possible. Learn to fix the copier, know the administrative assistant's needs, and pick the brains of the movers and shakers—especially those who think that no job is beneath them.

Your mind-set should be that you are in boot camp and that you want to learn and be exposed to six years of work in three years. Be thinking ahead about your educational options. Be ready to strike at the right time, when your current position can offer you nothing more, and then move on and make it happen.

DON'T BELIEVE THE HYPE

You were voted Most Likely to Succeed, and your parents believe you are the next Bill Gates. So what?

4

We all have one. Some are much larger than others. Some people hide theirs well, while some are extremely proud of it. It can be a person's greatest asset in business, but it also can cause problems in both career and personal life. If you haven't guessed what it is yet—it's your ego.

It doesn't matter if you are the CEO or the mail clerk; everyone has an ego. The term "ego" has a negative connotation, but I don't believe that having an ego is a bad thing at all. I hope everyone has an ego to some extent, because it can mean having confidence in who you are and what you do. To do something well, you will need to truly believe that you are capable.

> *"The higher the mountain you climb, the bigger the fall to the bottom."*

However, before you start patting yourself on the back and thinking about what a smart, intelligent, and charming person you are, remember that you need to control your ego and use it to your advantage. Unfortunately, a person's ego often gets in the way of his or her success and becomes a disadvantage to both personal life and career.

When I was twenty-three years old, I was receiving a lot of press in the media for my business. I was featured in numerous magazines and newspapers, and was interviewed on radio and television. If that was not enough, the amount of "friends" that I had was increasing. I was king of the world, and everyone was telling me so. One warning to all: the higher the mountain you climb, the bigger the fall to the bottom.

I became so obsessed with self-image that my old friends started having less to do with me. When you lose your true friends, it is not evident right away, because you have plenty of new "friends" hanging around. But these people may be there only to join you on the ride to the top of that mountain, and not to support you on the trip down. If you experience success, you will definitely make new "friends"; just don't forget who your true friends are.

My ego caused major problems within my business and my personal life. Bigger equated to better, or so I thought, and I hired more employees than were needed. I moved the company into a custom-built office space in a fancy building and made my personal office three times bigger than what I needed. Everything from the flooring to the furniture was excessive.

It would have been one thing if I was the only human being alive who had an ego—but as we all know, that is hardly the case. It did not occur to me that each of my employees had an ego as well. My company's first office had been one big room where our desks were close together, and it was a very intimate environment. Before the publicity onslaught and the plush new office, our work environment was at its very best. Moving into the new office space, however, made it clear that I was no longer at the same level as my employees. They were all in one large room together, while I now had a personal office with nice furniture and windows overlooking their workstations. Now I felt that everyone could see I was the boss. This did not go down well with my colleagues, and the person most affected by the new atmosphere was my right-hand man, who was key to our success thus far.

I later found out that this was a defining moment in our young company's existence. While it appeared that everything was going extremely well, once my ego reached new heights, my business began to have problems. I had enjoyed the most financial success when there was the least amount of fanfare, my staff size was small, and our office was simple.

As if the office space differential was not enough, once the publicity started coming in, one particular individual—my right-hand man—became even more disturbed by what was occurring. Despite his significant contribution, he was mentioned in only one of the many newspaper articles, television spots, and radio interviews that featured our company. Considering that my staff was the engine that made the car run, they obviously felt as though there was more to the success of our company than me—and they were 100 percent correct.

I failed miserably in sharing the recognition for our company's success. I treated that company as if it were my company, not our company. The more you make employees and coworkers feel that they *are* the company instead of merely working for the company, the more motivated they will become. Success will generally follow!

James T. Hackett
Chairman, CEO & President
ANADARKO PETROLEUM

The four biggest Career Killers I have witnessed are as follows:

1. Transparent ambition, especially if it outstrips one's ability
2. Not telling the truth
3. Choosing subordinates who cannot replace you (therefore rendering you unpromotable)
4. Shutting down others' views because of pride in one's own knowledge and judgment

If you are thinking to yourself that this does not apply to you because you are not in a management position, you are wrong. You have the power to be a leader on your own team and to create a better, more inclusive environment. My favorite concept regarding how to work with people comes from the book *The Dream Manager* by Matthew Kelly, who says, "Appreciation is the strongest currency in the corporate culture." I could not agree more.

In my own experiences, when a manager has complimented me or recognized me for my work, I received more satisfaction and more motivation to work harder than if I had been handed a $500 bonus. You are probably thinking right now, "If I had the option of choosing, I would pick the $500." But in reality, the most valuable of the two options is the recognition and praise.

Try it out—when someone on your team does something great, let that person know! Compliment her, praise her, and tell your teammates and your boss about it. Your input could be a key factor in increasing the morale and motivation of your team. If you are having trouble complimenting or praising people, you may benefit from this book's focus on keeping the ego in check.

> "*Let your success be everyone's success.*"

On the flip side, let's say you get recognized for putting together a great presentation for the vice president of your organization. Although you may have been the lead person on the project, your coworkers probably helped you with certain aspects or picked up your workload so you could focus more on the presentation. Praise and recognize all those who helped you achieve. Let your success be everyone's success, and take everyone who helped you get to the top with you.

Ray Jankowski
President & CEO
COMMUNITY HOSPITAL OF LONG BEACH

Acknowledging others for their good ideas or accomplishments is infinitely more important than calling attention to your own good ideas or accomplishments, no matter how wonderful you think that you might be.

Building trust among your peers and other coworkers and giving them the respect that they deserve is immensely important in the long run. Your own good ideas and accomplishments will earn recognition if they are truly worthy, and it's far more effective if people other than you call attention to your successes.

In other words, don't spend time "tooting your own horn"— despite historical advice to do so.

A few years ago I was at a conference of sales representatives. On one of the first nights of the conference, I was sitting at a table at the hotel bar. There were about eight of us, all of similar tenure in the same sales division within the company. Based on our company's sales commissions and bonuses, I suspect we all probably had incomes within a few thousand dollars of each other. As happens with most colleagues who get together, business and sales were the topics of conversation.

By nature, sales people can be a little self-absorbed. You almost have to be, because you need to be competitive and driven to succeed, and you must have confidence in yourself and your products. You would be hard-pressed to find a successful sales representative who did not think he is good at what he does. But I had learned some valuable lessons in my first business, when my ego got me in trouble. I learned that it's okay for people not to know of my successes.

That night in the hotel bar, the conversation soon changed to sales rankings, sales quotas, and how well we were performing. At this point I went into listener mode, nodding at those who tooted their own horn and giving praise to those who told success stories.

There were five hundred sales representatives in our sales sleeve, and we were ranked against one another. One rep was ranked 350th. Another was 190th, and another ranked as high as 94th. I was currently ranked 90th, which wasn't spectacular, but when I had walked into my territory, it was ranked 380th. I was proud of my turnaround in such a short amount of time. I had climbed in the rankings for nine straight months and was confident in continuing this trend. So as I listened to everyone, and as everyone talked about their accomplishments, the urge for me to do the same got stronger and stronger. The ego lives in all of us, and it got the best of me that night. Eventually I began talking about my sales success and mentioned my turnaround. I began my "me too" talk, because if everyone else was doing it, why shouldn't I?

Of course, as soon as I blew my own horn, I felt the realization wash over me: I should have just shut my mouth and not given in to the temptation of bragging. This continues to be a problem for me, but was more so in my first few years in business. I was so eager to prove my worth that I made sure everyone knew about my accomplishments. Just as Ray Jankowski says, I learned quickly that there is greater impact when people find out about your success on their own or from someone else—not from you! And yet years after I pledged to myself that I would follow these guidelines, I still fight the urge.

Dominic Orr
President & CEO
ARUBA NETWORKS, INC.

My top advice to young professionals is this: don't let job ranking and pay curves bother you in the short term.

Just focus on whom you serve—be they internal or external customers. Work hard to exceed their expectations, again and again…Over time, all other things will sort themselves out if you are clearly making an exceptional impact on your work environment.

When you think of a gigantic ego in the business world, one person usually comes to mind: Donald Trump. But I think "The Donald" is one of the best examples of how to use your ego appropriately and effectively. Trump's flashy self-confidence can be misconstrued as shameless self-absorption. But Trump knows he is good at what he does, and he does not hide the fact that he knows it.

"If you find yourself struggling to compliment someone, you may want to reevaluate your relationship with your ego."

More important, he does not take credit for all of his success. He constantly credits many of his employees for their great contributions to his organization. He also admits to having many mentors and to receiving guidance from a variety of people. Read any of Trump's books and you'll find that he is not above complimenting anyone. One of the biggest hindrances of an out-of-control ego is the inability to recognize greatness in others and to pay tribute to them. If you find yourself struggling to compliment someone, you may want to reevaluate your relationship with your ego.

So my best advice for all your personal and business endeavors is this: Don't Believe the Hype. Stay humble, and keep your true friends by your side at all times. There is a fine line between self-confidence and narcissism.

John Younger
President & CEO
ACCOLO, INC.

The working landscape is changing rapidly, and Career Killers today may not be Career Killers tomorrow.

For example, many people in their early twenties are posting things online about beer bashes, dates gone wrong, and a variety of extremely personal information...with pictures! What many people don't realize is that much of this will be accessible online until the sun goes nova. While certain things may be shrugged off as youthful indiscretions, future employers may make hiring decisions based on what they see, and the person applying for the job would never know the difference. In other words, there would be no way to prove whether the no-hire decision was based on pictures of that candidate running around scantily clad at Burning Man.

We actually had this happen with a candidate who was about ready to receive an offer of employment. Someone on the interview team discovered that she was into nude yoga. Because of this, the offer was never extended. Maybe in the future this sort of thing won't be a Career Killer—but I wouldn't bet on it.

ESTABLISH YOUR VALUES

Establish who you are now, so you protect yourself later.

5

The best way to start this chapter is with a story from Dr. Ned Hill, former dean of the Marriott School of Management at Brigham Young University. I cannot imagine a better story to show the importance of establishing your values and what you believe in early on—before you are in the middle of a situation in which you need them.

Ned C. Hill, PhD

Former Dean of the Marriott School of Management
BRIGHAM YOUNG UNIVERSITY

twitter me
nedhill44

Bob (not his real name) graduated at the top of his class at Brigham Young University's Marriott School of Management. He was one of those unusual students who had everything: talent, personality, drive, an attractive and talented wife, and a little one-year-old boy born during his MBA program.

Not surprisingly, Bob landed a plum job at an investment bank in the San Francisco Bay Area. With his generous signing package and excellent salary (not to mention the promise of a hefty bonus at the end of the year), he rented a nice condo, bought a new car, purchased some furniture, and began his promising career as an investment banker.

Not too many months into his budding career, Bob's group leader came to him and invited him to take a major role in an important initial public offering (IPO). No other young associate was given anywhere near this level of responsibility. It was an exhilarating feeling. The catch was, he had to shade certain unsavory problems about the financial condition of the issuing company. Bob's leader let him know that they would have to do this in order for the IPO to get the price they needed in this particular market. "It's what we all do!" the boss assured Bob.

Ned recommends *Seven Habbits of Highly Effective People* by Stephen Covey

Bob was shocked. He had always thought of this firm as one with high ethical standards. He searched his soul. Maybe this was what he had to do to succeed. Is this what everyone was expected to do?

He wrestled with this conflict for several days and talked it over with his wife. They had so many financial commitments. Could they afford to give up his income and a promising opportunity at one of the best-known investment banks in the country?

They finally came to the conclusion that, come what may, they could not bear to live with a wounded conscience. They had to think of their son—could they explain their decision to him someday when he faced an ethical challenge? Could they face themselves, knowing that they personally were committed to living a life with integrity?

Bob visited with his boss and asked to be taken off the IPO. He offered to work on any other projects the bank had—but not one that compromised what he thought was right.

His boss was not happy with Bob's reaction. He thought Bob must lack "market toughness." "If you're not going to work on this IPO, I'll see to it you won't work anywhere in this bank."

Bob resigned.

It took a lot of courage to face his boss. It took a lot of courage to face an end to a promising career and large income stream. But Bob and his wife made a tough decision and stuck by it.

Bob was without work for several months. They had to move in with family while Bob searched for another job. He finally found one with a firm that allowed him to stick by his standards of honesty and integrity. He is now doing very well in that firm, has several more children, and has a clear conscience that lets him sleep well at night. This couple faced a huge challenge and made a tough decision.

Most managers proclaim that they have integrity. They may even understand how integrity applies to business management—intellectually, at least.

The real test comes when one has large financial obligations, the promise of high income in the future, and colleagues who expect one to fall in line with their expectations. It's important to understand that Bob and his wife essentially had decided how they would respond to ethical challenges before they actually faced them. The pressure to behave unethically was balanced by their own moral integrity.

My advice to young professionals: think carefully about ethics before you find yourself facing the actual situation in your job. Know beforehand how you will respond to those who ask you to violate your ethical standards.

Will you violate your ethical standards?

There is a corollary to this advice: keep your debts and other financial obligations as low as you can, so you do not feel pressured into actions that compromise your ethical standards. The data illustrates that most companies and individuals who are involved in financial frauds also have excessively high personal debt levels.

Dr. Hill brings up an excellent point regarding debts and financial obligations. About six years ago, while working on one of my business ventures, I got myself in some financial trouble. I had never felt the amount of pressure or uneasiness that I did at that time. Luckily, guidance from sound business advisers and trusted family members helped me get out of that situation without compromising my values. However, the amount of anxiety and stress I experienced over finances is something I hope never to feel again, especially now that I can see how easily it influences one's decision-making process.

Since getting married, my wife and I have strived to avoid any debt except the mortgage on our house. By not overextending ourselves in terms of our financial obligations, we have found that it is easier to make sound moral and ethical decisions in our lives. Think about it: if a person is $2,000 in debt and one day accidentally receives in the mail a cashier's check for $500, that person may have second thoughts about finding the rightful home for that check. And for most of us, the stakes are even higher; it is scary to think that the average American household has $8,500 in credit card debt. With that much pressure on America's shoulders, I would venture to say that debt—rather than ethical standards—is influencing a lot of decision-making processes.

When establishing your values and what you stand for, consider it an opportunity to evaluate who you are and what you want to contribute to the world around you. If you are offered a job by a company that has a reputation for doing something you do not agree with (outsourcing, child labor, etc.), then by accepting that position you may be walking into a future ethical or moral dilemma. If you have a clear understanding of your values, it will be easier to walk away from an opportunity that could cause a problem in the future.

BLOG ME:
ypsuccess.com
Share your
thoughts.

Christopher J. Calhoun
Cofounder & CEO
CYTORI THERAPEUTICS, INC.

When considering your career, choose wisely, as you will likely spend more time doing this than just about anything else in your adult life.

One approach is what my friend Ralph Holmes, MD, used to tell me—he called it "the seventy-year rule." Imagine you are now seventy years old and reflecting on your life, perhaps sharing your accomplishments and experiences with your grandchildren. How would your career choices be positioned? What contributions would you be proud of? Did you make a difference in the world? To certain people? To science or humanity in general? Would you share this experience with enthusiasm about something important and meaningful that you did, or would it be a footnote to your overall life story? Somehow, this perspective changes the focus from earning money to finding something you can be passionate about, something you can be proud of...something you can tell your grandkids about.

As with Bob in the story that Dr. Hill shares, a person who knows her values can feel safe in making decisions about work and employment. If an employer asks an individual to do something that she feels is wrong, not having a pile of debt clouding the decision-making process can tip the balance in favor of her integrity.

For a lot of people, values can be defined by their religious beliefs. As a practicing Christian, I find that most of my values come from my faith. Jim Hackett of Anadarko Petroleum and Jonathan Reckford of Habitat for Humanity are led by their religious beliefs, and I admire and thank these men for sharing openly about them.

James T. Hackett
Chairman, President & CEO
ANADARKO PETROLEUM

My one piece of advice for young professionals is to realize as early as possible that God gave each of us particular talents and that our duty is to act with integrity and serve others. Remarkable things can happen to all of us personally and professionally if we carry this attitude into our lives. In terms of professional conduct, we should strive to do more than is asked (especially in our early career); make time for personal health maintenance (throughout one's career); find a partner (or a good friend) with whom we can share our fears, delights, and ambitions and who can also be a check on our ambitions and behaviors; never become too proud (it is a guarantee of ultimate failure); engage in community and philanthropic activities (to remind us of the misfortune of others, relative to our blessings); and practice prayer—there will be a time where no one can be depended upon other than our Maker.

Speaking your mind, politely, is good.

Young people should always assume that speaking their mind—politely—is good. Older people will admire the backbone and courage it shows. Personal courage is hugely important the further one advances in a career. Putting your job on the line for a good cause is an immense privilege. There are moments of truth in which one's character can be tested.

Planning and preparation truly matter. Kindness to others is important, but don't mistake this as weakness, or as the need to sympathize with improper behavior in others. Giving people honest feedback is critical. Approaching others to help you with your development is not a sign of weakness. True friends challenge their friends or colleagues rather than always agreeing with them.

Not everyone has religious tenets that mold their value system. But just as Christians hold dear the values of Jesus Christ, you can find leaders or mentors in your own life after whom you can model your values.

Jonathan T. M. Reckford
Chief Executive Officer
HABITAT FOR HUMANITY INTERNATIONAL

My career did not exactly turn out the way I had planned. In fact, one of my key learnings is that the more I tried to plan or control my future, the worse the result. I have found more fulfillment and success in those times when I was less focused on myself and more focused on just getting things done.

As a follower of Jesus, I aspire to be a servant leader. That is a radically countercultural definition of success in a society that screams, "Happiness will come from owning more stuff!" rather than from forming one's character from the right stuff. Oscar Wilde wrote that each action of the common day either makes or unmakes our character. You have to be clear on who you want to be before you worry about what you are going to do.

Often we can see God's hand at work in our lives more clearly in the rearview mirror. I can now see how what seemed like a random career path was actually getting me ready for my dream job. Working for Habitat for Humanity has allowed me to merge vocation and avocation, to take what I learned in the business world and blend it with the passion and sense of purpose I experienced serving in a church.

My grandmother, Millicent Fenwick, was a formidable and iconoclastic congresswoman from New Jersey. She had lots of advice, but the most useful was her regular quoting of Micah 6:8, which

> Where do your passion and skills intersect?

says: "What does the Lord require of you? To act justly and to love mercy, and to walk humbly with your God." If you are not sure what to do, that is a pretty good place to start. I am still trying to live into that call.

So my advice for young professionals is to figure out how you are wired, what you were born to do. Reflect on those times in your life when you felt a great sense of accomplishment (which may not necessarily be something for which you won praise or adulation) and home in on what Arthur Miller called your "motivated abilities"— where your passion and skills intersect. Then, regardless of your faith or motivation, figure out how to use those abilities to make the world a little more just, merciful, and filled with grace. It won't be easy, but it will be good.

When you establish your own values, you establish the values to which you will hold your employees if you become a manager or own your own business. Your personal values can help shape the organization that you are a part of or that you want to run one day.

Your values are extremely important even beyond yourself. As you grow as a professional and a leader, your values have the ability to affect others, in both good ways and bad. Bill Hermann explains how the founder of Plante & Moran, Frank Moran, created a sound, ethical environment by setting specific values for the company more than fifty years ago.

Bill Hermann

Firm Managing Partner

PLANTE & MORAN, PLLC

Years ago, Plante & Moran made a choice about the kind of firm we would be. We chose to optimize rather than maximize our profits. I can't tell you when that choice was made, and maybe the word "choice" is inappropriate, because that mentality simply goes to the core of who we are. We aren't a firm that's focused solely on the bottom line. A lot of firms find success with that mentality, but it doesn't work for us. Instead, we continuously make investments—investments that may not pay off tomorrow, next month, or next year—but ones that we feel are in the best interest of our staff and the firm.

The key to success is focusing on the balance of all these elements. Doing the right things for the right reasons allows you to obtain the right results. This belief is visualized in an icon that we call our "Wheel of Progress." The Wheel demonstrates how our values interconnect and allow the entire organization, and all the clients we serve, to prosper and thrive. The Wheel of Progress reads like this: "Good work attracts good clients, who are able to pay good fees, which will attract good staff, who are capable of doing good work." Start anyplace on the wheel, and the result is the same. Frank Moran designed the wheel fifty years ago, and we still use it as a core foundation for our strategic planning and people development initiatives.

"*Doing the right things for the right reasons allows you to obtain the right results.*"

A friend of mine—I'll call him John—worked as a salesperson for a manufacturing company. John loved being in sales and loved the products he was selling. However, sales results for his region had been suffering and his manager was applying more pressure to his entire sales team to pick up the pace.

The company had recently released a newer version of one of its most popular products. The newer product was more efficient and gave John's company a huge edge over the competition. It was just what the company needed to give a shot in the arm to its sales. John was very excited when he began getting sales orders from companies where he previously could not get in the door.

Most of John's current clients also began buying the newer version of the product. But as time passed, John noticed that one of his oldest and most reliable clients had not been ordering any of the new product. The CEO of this company and John shared a great relationship. They enjoyed business lunches and even had gone on a hunting trip together, and the CEO treated John more as a favorite nephew than a vendor.

After deciding to put some numbers together to present to this company and its CEO, John stopped by his own boss's office to verify a few figures. He explained matters and asked the questions he needed to ask. His boss got a serious look on his face and said, "Let's not rock the boat here. This CEO has always been a fan of our current product, so I don't think we need to push the new version on him." He remembered that John had visited with the CEO and showed him the new version, and said, "If he wanted to make the change, he would have."

It was true that John's company had released the new version of the product to attract new customers, and it was not specifically intended for current customers who were happy enough with the old product. However, John felt obligated to make sure the CEO was fully aware of the benefits of the new version. On the other hand, his boss had instructed him not to do so. What was John supposed to do in this situation?

This brings me back to my business ethics course in college, when we talked about obligations. The question you have to ask is "Who was John obligated to?" He had an obligation to his manager. He had an obligation to his company, because ultimately his responsibility was to make his company more profitable. He had an obligation to his client, who trusted him and assumed that John was looking out for his best interests. John also had an obligation to his wife and family, to provide a good income.

BLOG ME:
ypsuccess.com
Share your thoughts.

As difficult as it was to see my friend in a tough situation, it interested me to explore an ethical dilemma that could provoke thought and discussion. The correct answer depends on which obligation held the most value for John. There is no right or wrong answer unless John were to go against his values. What would you do? Take some time to think about it. John eventually decided to go ahead and approach his CEO client with the new version of the product. He also found out that the CEO had recently been approached by a competitor, so John's timing was perfect. The CEO was weighing his decision based on the older product, but when the new product was presented, he opted for it and quickly dismissed the competition. John's boss was pleased when he heard what had happened (although with a little egg on his face). John valued his integrity with his client, as well as his integrity with his company. He knew that if he compromised once, his boss might ask him to do it again. It was his opportunity to display his values to his clients and his company and boss.

Neil Nicoll
President & CEO
YMCA OF THE USA

Treat everyone with respect. Learn about their interests, families, jobs, etc. Do not expect people to have great interest in you and your priorities if you cannot take interest in them.

Base your decisions on what is in the best interest of those you serve. It seems obvious, but when the going gets tough, don't allow yourself to become self-serving.

A long-term commitment to doing right rather than what is expedient is the foundation for a healthy career.

In the chapter "Are You Prepared for Success?" I introduced you to the term Career Killers. For a long time that was my favorite way to describe an action or attitude that can ruin you professionally—until Tom Darrow of Talent Connections shared with me the term FUBR (pronounced "foobar"). It stands for "fouled up beyond repair" (though Tom points out that "fouled" can be replaced by another particular F-word). I now love that term and use it more often than Career Killer. Tom pointed out a PG-rated version of the term: CLM, which stands for "career-limiting move." Both are great—very appropriate for our discussion—but FUBR is the one that has stuck with me.

Tom Darrow

Founder & Principal, TALENT CONNECTIONS, LLC
Founder & Principal, CAREER SPA, LLC

The biggest FUBR is to have a reputation as someone who can't be trusted.

Sometimes, things one does in one's personal life can cause this effect by leaking over into a person's business reputation. Heavy drinking, carousing, mean-spirited actions, etc.—the word will spread, and it will kill your career.

So start thinking now about what is important to you—what line you will or won't cross in order succeed. That way, you'll be more likely to recognize it when you come upon it in the future—and to make choices that you can live with.

Clint Severson

President & CEO
ABAXIS, INC.

First you need to start with a vision of what you want to be—what you want to have or accomplish, or where you want to finish in the pecking order of life. This is the simple part. That is, if you are enlightened enough to know you can do almost anything you set your mind to, and if you are willing to pay the price to achieve success.

Once you have your objectives, you need to set the goals that will aid you in getting there. And you need all the assistance you can get in setting these goals. After receiving advice from all your friends and relatives, you should formulate your plan and set your goals.

Once your goals are set, keep at it. Never give up. Keep solving the problems, one at a time, with focused persistence. When you're finished with one goal, go to the next one.

Setbacks give you time to reevaluate your strategy.

Patience is key to success. You will be doing things you have never done before, so how long it takes you will remain unknown. Let setbacks give you time to reevaluate your strategy and, if you are off course, work on a correction. Seek out a mentor to assist you. Keep focused on the goal. When you make mistakes—and you will—or find that your assumptions are wrong, fix it. Fast. The sooner it is fixed, the faster you can get on with productive activities.

You will be surprised how much you can achieve with vision, focus, persistence, patience, and the discipline to fix mistakes fast.

DEFINE SUCCESS USING THE FIVE Fs

Family, Faith, Fitness, Finances, and Fun—as taught by an entrepreneur, philanthropist, and fan of life

6

In 2003, I was to introduce myself and Young Execs to a different organization I had joined, one that featured business leaders and former professional athletes in San Antonio. All new members of this organization were expected to introduce themselves at their first monthly luncheon. I was a little nervous about what to say. These individuals had experienced incredible things in their lifetime, and I was noticeably younger than most of them. But I decided this was my opportunity to make an impression and show them I could be just another "one of the guys" (even though I was nowhere near where they were, neither in my life nor in my career).

At the luncheons, the featured speaker took over the podium after the new member introductions. I felt pretty good about my introduction and walked away thinking that these gentlemen would surely accept me as one of their own. By the time the luncheon was over, however, I had realized that I would be lucky if anybody would remember my name. That's because the thirty minutes following my introduction had changed my life in a dramatic fashion.

I had heard of the speaker in name only, but I was familiar with the fact that he formerly owned a business that was sold to a gentleman I knew. His name was Roy Terracina, and he had grown up in inner-city Chicago, the son of a tight-knit Italian Catholic family. He was sharply dressed, looked to be in his early fifties, and was in tip-top physical shape. He was not intimidating by any means, but when he walked to the front of the room, there was a definite presence.

After listening to Roy, I knew that this was one of the most important messages that any of us would ever hear. Instead of trying to remember (and possibly butcher) everything that Roy said that day, I asked Roy to contribute to this book, so that every reader can hear the speech I heard that day.

Roy Terracina
President
SUNSHINE VENTURES

I start out every speech in the same way. When we get to the end, I want you one of you to ask me about the Trinity speech. But right now I'm going to read this poem to you, and I'd like you to take it to heart because it means a lot to me. It's actually sitting in a frame right outside my office.

> *If I Had My Life to Live Over*
> *I'd dare to make more mistakes next time.*
> *I'd relax, I would limber up.*
> *I would be sillier than I have been this trip.*
> *I would take fewer things seriously.*
> *I would take more chances.*
> *I would climb more mountains and swim more rivers.*
> *I would eat more ice cream and less beans.*
> *I would perhaps have more actual troubles, but I'd have fewer imaginary ones.*

You see, I'm one of those people who live sensibly and sanely, hour after hour, day after day.

Oh, I've had my moments,
And if I had it to do over again,
I'd have more of them.
In fact, I'd try to have nothing else.
Just moments, one after another, instead of living so many years
ahead of each day.

I'm going to stop there for a moment. This is our moment. Okay? This next hour is our moment. Hopefully you'll be able to remember it ten years from now. But it's our moment. So, let's block all these other things going on. You've got an exam next week, laundry to do tonight, a date later, it's Valentine's Day. Skip it.

Let's take this moment.

I've been one of those people who never goes anywhere without a
thermometer, a hot water bottle, a raincoat and a parasol.
If I had to do it again, I would travel lighter than I have.
If I had my life to live over,
I would start barefoot earlier in the spring and stay that way later
in the fall.
I would go to more dances.
I would ride more merry-go-rounds.
I would pick more daisies.
That is what I'd do if I had my life to live over again.
But you see, I don't.

This woman was eighty-five.

I just spent the last week with my father, who is eighty-three. I have to tell you, he is the most energetic eighty-three-year-old you've ever been around in your life. I buy my dad a new car every three years, and he always buys a Nissan Maxima. That's his car of choice.

I called him up two months ago and he said, "You know, I've had this car thirty-seven months. We've missed. It's time to get me a new one."

I told him, "You go to the dealer and you call me when you get there."

He went to the car dealer and called me up and said, "They're screwing me."

"What do you mean?"

"Well, they said I have too many miles on this one."

I asked, "Well, too many miles? How many miles do you have on it?"

He said, "115,000."

Put that in your brain. Thirty-seven months, 115,000 miles, and he's eighty-three years old. It's a good news/bad news story. I want him driving as much as he can, but 38,000 miles a year for an eighty-three-year-old guy? He's driving. He still works every day.

What did we learn from the poem? Obviously, live this life. We can't predict what's going to happen. My motto would be to have as much fun as you can. Make every day fun. You don't have to worry about what's going on around you. You can't control most of it anyway.

I'm going to open up my heart, my life to you a little bit. And hopefully you'll learn a little bit from it, or a little about me, or maybe some things will trickle down and help you understand that I'm not any different from you.

I was a first-generation college student. I'm very proud of it. But I always talk about some feelings that I've had in my life—feelings that I couldn't begin to even think that anyone else has had. I'm sure people have, but I like to think mine are special.

And one of them is, that I was divorced at age twenty-seven from my childhood sweetheart, an Italian Catholic from Chicago, like I was. I was raised in the city. Everyone there was Italian.

We had three children, and getting divorced from her was a dev-astating thing to me because I never in my wildest dreams thought I'd be divorced. To me, when you marry someone, you marry someone... It's a feeling I can't begin to explain.

The second feeling gets me every time. I held my mother's hand as she took her last breath.

To me, that's enough to say, right? She died of cancer twenty years ago. You have only one mother. The only positive thing about her passing is that it has enabled me to have a greater relationship with my father than I had prior to that. My mother was a very strong-willed person, you see, and I was her only son.

The third feeling was to be able to watch my young boys being born. You see, I have five children. My oldest is thirty-nine, and my youngest is seventeen. And back when we had the thirty-nine- and thirty-eight-year-old sons and my daughter, who is thirty-six, they didn't let the dad go into the delivery room or anything like that. You sat out on the couch. For the second son, I can remember the doctor coming over and waking me up and saying, "You just had another son."

"Okay," I said.

By the time I got down to my last two boys, who are named Peter and Paul, they allowed us in the delivery room. And to watch the birth of a child, it was just a miracle. At least to a simple man who doesn't know much about all that stuff. To watch my sons being born was a very special thing to me, so I had to give them strong, spiritual names like Peter and Paul.

For years I would make this speech and talk only of these three feelings. Then in the year 2001 I got a call from my then-wife; she had been diagnosed with cancer. I really thought she was going to die. She didn't. But I kept thinking of my two sons, who were nine and eleven, and what they would have to go through if their mother died. That cancer caused lots of other things to happen. One of which was, we ended up divorced. I blame the cancer for it all. She wouldn't, but I think the cancer started a chain of events.

I have to believe that when you are used to being somewhat in control of things, then God taps you on the shoulder and says, "You've got cancer," you realize you're probably not in control. Never did the words "Thy will be done" mean so much to me as when she was sick. It's whatever the Lord is going to pick. And he chose to keep her alive.

So those are my open feelings that I can't really begin to explain, but I try. You can't feel them unless you're inside of me.

I was raised in inner-city Chicago, probably like a lot of you—in a neighborhood where there wasn't a whole lot of wealth. There weren't a whole lot of people with big jobs. No doctors, no lawyers. People worked in factories, worked as policemen, or worked on the bus. That was my neighborhood.

My father was a self-made guy. He was an entrepreneur. So I had probably a little bit of a different vision just because I saw him going to his own company every day, and he ran a retail store.

I was raised half a block from my grandparents, across the street from the convent and across the alley from the rectory. There was a church right there, and my grandparents were right next to that. So you can see all the churches were a big part of my life as a child, as was my family. I had lunch with my grandmother and grandfather every day of my life until I was thirteen.

In fact, until I was thirteen, I didn't know that there was anyone BUT an Italian family. That's all there was. It was my life, you see. You're in an inner city. One square mile around you, and everyone in that one square mile was Italian Catholic. It wouldn't be so different over here on Zarzamora Street, I'm sure.

Culture was very important.

Some people in this room play sports, let's say. I chose a sport that was very different than everyone else. I was a prizefighter. You know, that means getting in a ring with another guy and boxing. It taught me a whole lot about life. Because life is one-on-one, to me. It's win/lose. There's no in between. If any of you choose to go play the game of life and just sort of get involved in it, you're cheating yourself. You play it to win. And winning can mean a lot of things, but at least go at it with a passion. But if you look around, there's lots of people who don't have passion. They just do life. They get up in the morning and do their thing. They go to bed and get up the next day and it's the same way. Well, I firmly believe that every day should be lived as though it's your last. In fact, I believe in it so much, I'm comfortable that if today is my last, then I know where I'm going. That's where my faith is. So I live every day with that kind of vigor. Just let me do whatever I can today to make it a great day, not only for myself but for others around me.

But that was a part of boxing. I was a Golden Gloves champion when I was fourteen. This goes back a long ways, to 1960. I boxed all the way until I was twenty years old, and that was my thing.

I was in a street gang. Some of you may have been in a gang, may know what that's like. I carried a gun. I was part of a gang. That was just what my life was. All my friends were gang members, so guess what? I was a gang member. You're pushed. You're motivated by your peers, as you all know, right? Your peers are what challenge you to different things. Well, my peers were going in that direction. And for whatever reason, when I was a freshman in high school I chose to go to a different school. I just didn't want to be in that environment all the time. So I went to the fancy school. It would be as though somebody, some of you here, chose to go to a prestigious private school in an upper-class area. You can imagine that if you were raised on the wrong side of the tracks and you went to this private school, you never fit. But you go out there and play the game every day. You know, I wore a coat and tie and went into the school every morning like it was the place I was supposed to be, but every night I went back to my neighborhood. I put on the gloves and trained for a couple of hours, put my gun in my pocket, and walked outside.

That was my life. I met my first wife when I was sixteen. That kept me out of some trouble, because I was dating instead of hanging with my friends. I was out on a date a lot at night. I'd still meet my friends at midnight or one, but at least it kept me out of the trouble that happened in between.

And then came time for college. I graduated—and this is something that I am not proud of—something like 275th out of 285 in my high school class. Now, you could take a snapshot and understand why. Not that I was stupid, but I was coming from here, going to school there. I never fit. So my grades just kind of did enough to get me out. So I got out of high school. It was such a fine high school that I had no problem getting into a college; it wasn't necessarily the college I wanted, but it was a college. So I went to school in Louisville, Kentucky, for a year. Got my grades to where they had to be and then transferred to Marquette—now my alma mater—where I really wanted to go to school. Marquette University, a fine Catholic Jesuit school in Milwaukee, about 80 miles from home. So it was closer to get back. So close, and yet not so close that I couldn't do my own thing.

It was about that time that I made the decision to get married. So here I am, a college junior, married to my childhood sweetheart. I still had a year to go in school, and I'll never forget coming home from one of my classes my senior year in September, and she put dinner on the table and said, "Well, guess what? We're going to have a baby."

My first son was born nine months and nine days after my marriage, so we didn't have a whole lot of time to get to know each other.

The second son was born thirteen months later. So I have two sons barely into my marriage, two years into my marriage.

I got a job in the banking business immediately out of college. I'd majored in finance. It's always been my life, numbers. I love numbers, so I became a finance major. Immediately after graduating and starting a job (and raising children at the same time), I decided to get an MBA at night. So I was working full time during the day, fathering two children, being a husband, and going to grad school at night.

I had a young man tell me the other day he was having trouble juggling school and life and I said to him, "Look, how would you like to juggle two children, a job, school, and life? You know, I mean, you can do it. It's all a matter of what you think you can do."

I got to be about twenty-seven or twenty-eight years old and that marriage imploded. It was a sad thing, because then we had a daughter as well. I majored in business, then started having success in the business world—and the rewards in business are what? What happens if you are a successful businessman? You make money and work long hours, but your reward is money. And I've always felt that's a very shallow reward. But it's the choice I made, to be a businessman.

Let's say I'd chosen to be this poet, Nadine Stair. How good would I feel if my poem got published in a book? In fact, hers is published in a book, and the book is called *If Had to Live My Life Over Again*. Wouldn't that be a great feeling? So if I got my poem published—or if you're a doctor, and you're a cancer doctor, you're saving people's lives. What a great reward!

But I chose business, and my reward was money, and when I visited with my friends we kinda looked at each other and went, "How much did you make last year? And by the way, are you still leasing that jet? How about that new car you got?"

I find that to be very shallow. So that's philosophically where I come from. From that standpoint, I wished at times I had chosen something else. I know now that I could have chosen something else, because I'm not really a businessman anymore. I sold my business fourteen years ago, and the Lord's given me an opportunity to do something else. And the something else is not being involved in business but talking about my faith. Talking to young people like you and being a great dad and a great grandfather. I have eight grandchildren. So I have to be a great grandfather. I have to spend a lot of time with them. And be a great son. And be a great servant. Those are the things that I am going to be measured on. I hope. Not how much money I've made in my life, because even though the stock market may be up today—I know it's up, I know that's a good thing, but it doesn't matter. It really doesn't matter, but we have to have a way to measure ourselves, and that's what I'm measuring myself on now I guess.

So let's go back to this life. So I'm moving along as a divorced dad, became the treasurer of a big public company in Wisconsin. I had the kind of job that I would bet any of you could look out today and say, "Gosh, at age thirty-four or thirty-five if I could be anything…" Well, I was the treasurer of a billion-and-a-half-dollar company. My office was on the top floor of the biggest building in Milwaukee, Wisconsin. I looked out at Lake Michigan where the sailboats were sailing, the sky was blue. Pick up the phone: "Is the limousine ready? I need to go to New York today." Go downstairs, get in the limo. It takes me to the airport. Private jet flies me to New York for lunch. Come back home so I can be with my kids at night.

That was my life. And in one day it changed just that quickly. The change was that my sons from my first marriage came into my office. My office, by the way, was incredible. It was just a neat, neat place.

They said, "Dad! Mom tells us that if you ever leave Milwaukee, we can come and live with you."

"What did you say?"

"If you leave Milwaukee, we can come and live with you."

"Well, guys, if that's the case, I'm going to find a way to get us out of here."

"And by the way, Dad, Angie can't come."

My daughter couldn't come.

"She's only nine, and Mom thinks it would better if we left and she stayed with her."

Okay, so I'd get into that one and see what I could do with that.

So I came to San Antonio and found a business. Actually, I found a business and then came to San Antonio to look and see if I could buy this business. It was a little business on Bandera and 410, and it was called Sterling Bakery. It was a manufacturer of bakery goods for the military, primarily for Lackland Air Force Base, and then it sold rations, food that soldiers eat, to the military. It was a little-bitty business. About eight million in sales, had about 150 employees, but I could afford to buy it.

So I got in the plane with my father. Why would you get in the plane with your father? He's not a baker. He's certainly a good businessman, but he's my father. I wanted his advice. So I flew down there with him. We looked at the company, and I decided I would buy it. I brought some partners with me and I bought this business.

Now, it's 1984, so most of you weren't even born, but I came to San Antonio with two young teenage sons. I borrowed seven million dollars to buy a business, and I was single. I called this young lady up and I said, "How would you like to move to Texas and help me raise my children?" We had been dating for seven years.

She said to me, "The only way I'll move is if we get married."

"Get married? Why would you want to ruin this perfectly good relationship? We're having a great relationship. Now what are we going to do if we get married? Well, you'll have to give me a few days to think about it."

I was staying in a little hotel on 410. I'll never forget it. It was called the Lexington Motor Inn. I don't know what it's called now. I called her back in three days with what was the best decision I made in my life. I said, "Would you marry me?"

So put that in perspective. In seven weeks, I bought a business for seven million dollars, got custody of my two sons, got married, and moved to what felt like the end of the Earth. San Antonio, Texas. Are you kidding me? I lived in Chicago, moved to Milwaukee and was in a high-rise office building, and now my company was on Bandera and 410, in the industrial park. That was my office. So lots of things changed very quickly.

The peak in my business was, like I said, we were making food for soldiers. The order came from the government to make as many as I could. That would be any businessman's biggest dream—a phone call that says, "Make as many as you can."

"What am I going to charge you for them?'

"Don't worry about it. You'll figure it out later, but just keep making them."

I went from about two hundred employees to eighteen hundred in seven weeks. But my mission was to make food for guys who might get killed. And it drove me crazy. People kept telling me, "Boy, you must be successful. How does it feel to be so successful?" You know what? It felt like shit, because what if a kid got killed? My assistant's son was a frontline marine. He's the first one there. Every day, I'd go into the company and think, you know, she's going to tell me her kid got killed. Here we are in San Antonio and guess what? A lot of moms have kids in the military here. This is a military city. I'd go down to my platform, and I'd hear "My son Billy is over there right now." It just drove me crazy. I would end up in a shrink's office once a week dealing with "success." That's how I knew that when it ended, I had to get out—because if it ever happened again, I would probably have gone crazy.

Another snapshot of that moment: my oldest son Joe was twenty years old during Desert Storm. Back when I was a young man and a war broke out, they started drafting people. All I could think was, I'm making money off the military and they're going to take my kid. And my other son, by the way, was nineteen—so twenty and nineteen. Not a good time. So it was the wrong business for me. How does my faith play into that? I have to believe in the feeling that making money was not my motivation.

Why did I move here? My kids have always been the reason. Lots of other ways to make money, but I wanted to be here with my sons. By the way, my daughter came to live with us later. She came when she was a high school sophomore. She came because my son Peter was born; she now has a son whose name is Peter, too. She wanted to be with her family. By the way, they are half brother and sister. You'd never hear any of my children saying it that way: "half." Doesn't happen.

We travel together every year, somewhere, all of us.

So anyway, the business did slowly at first, but then it did very well. It grew to be a nice company. I sold it in 1993. My mother died in 1987, and Peter was born in 1988, and Paul in 1990.

So life went fine at that point. Sold Sterling and I thought, "Well, I'll go find something else to do." I was forty-seven years old. Certainly there's more to life than running this company. There must be another one.

Right around that time, a Catholic priest walked into my office and said, "Roy, my brother went to school with you at Marquette. I'm here in San Antonio trying to work with kids who are at risk," because you know San Antonio in '94, '93 had the highest drive-by shooting rate in the country. He said, "I came from Detroit doing the same kind of work. I'm going to work with kids in high schools like Brackenridge, South San, Page Middle."

I said, "Father, I'm here. I'm going to help you. I'm selling my company. I need something to do."

So I got involved with him, became chairman of the board, raised a bunch of money. It was called something like Life's Directions, and we proceeded to turn some things around in the city by getting kids that needed to be motivated by their peers in the same room with other kids.

I would venture to say that if I brought one of these kids who was just visiting with me, he would motivate all of you, because he's from San Antonio and he's now working on his PhD at Our Lady of the Lake University. He's had a lot of hurdles, but a hurdle is just that— it's just a little bump in the road, and you go over it, right? Don't let it stop you.

So we were bringing those kids together, and those kids would say, "I got kicked out of class today. I'm having trouble with my parents. They're idiots."

You would visit with another kid who was a straight-A student: "My parents are idiots, too."

That's right, all parents of teenagers are idiots. That's just the way it goes. Well, you find out they have the same problems, and sooner or later all the kids were working together to help each other out—to get their grades up and stay out of trouble at night—and it worked in the city.

Father Alex has since left and gone on to do some more work in Birmingham, Alabama. At the time, though, I was at a charity of my choice. There's lots of charities, but I was passionate about that one because it dealt with troubled youth. The point is that it took me to another level. It got me away from my business and into something that I was very passionate about: helping kids. And I did that until the year 2000, and since then I've had a wife with cancer, and here I am today.

That's the short version of a lot of things going on. But know that I am passionate about life. I spent a lot of time with a lot of young people. Typical day can range from anything from…who knows, all sorts of things might happen when you're working with young people.

How many of you have seen the movie *The Ringer*? In *The Ringer* is a young African-American guy named Jimmy. The real Jimmy is from San Antonio. Jimmy is my sixth child. Jimmy is a Special Olympic athlete, whose real name is Leonard Flowers.

Leonard entered my life at age nineteen. He's now thirty-five. Every day he calls me and says, "What do you need around the house? How can I help you today? I've got a problem with my taxes." Leonard has real-life problems; he has a learning disability. He lives about a mile and a half from my house and comes there twice a week, and I'd venture to say that every other time he gets lost. He just doesn't have the normal…He is my sixth child. I spend a lot of time with Leonard. I get more out of that than when I was meeting with some big businessman.

FAMILY
FAITH
FUN
FITNESS
FINANCES

My son, who is a freshman at Texas Christian University, wrote his essay to get into TCU on what he learned from Leonard Flowers. What does a young man learn from a Special Olympics athlete? Lots of things, right? And obviously, it helped get him in the university, because he wasn't the best of students. But he had the best semester of his life during his freshman year in college. I can't imagine how he did it, and I'm proud of him.

My message would be, life takes lots of turns, lots of changes. Be ready to have fun every day. I believe in the five Fs. I call them my five Fs. And one of them, the biggest in many ways, is my family. It will always be the most important.

My faith. Right?

Having fun. Got it?

Fitness. There's not a day that goes by that I don't work out. When I leave here today I'll get to the hotel at two thirty. Promise, promise, promise. Gotta work out.

Finances. Obviously if you don't have your finances in order, you couldn't do all these other things. I couldn't work out at two thirty if I didn't have my financial life in order. So it's important, but it's not a priority. It's not what you aim at. You aim at finding the thing you are passionate about, and you'll be successful. People like teachers are the biggest givers in the world. People who teach. They have to be passionate about it, because it certainly doesn't give the kind of monetary rewards that are due to them.

How about someone who teaches Special Olympics athletes? What a calling that's got to be. That's a tough sell. How do you teach them? How do you teach someone who can't learn? Well, they learn, but not the same way we learn.

So that's it. I'm going to let you all ask me lots of questions. Let me tell you about the speech at Trinity University first. That may open the door to some things.

I made a similar speech there just last week, and at the end of it, a young man came to me and said, "Mr. Terracina, it seems as though you leave yourself very open, and a lot of people must take advantage of you because of that. How do you handle it when they take advantage of you?"

I'm at Trinity, a nonreligious school of sorts, right? My son went there, so I know—my oldest son.

I said to him, "Young man, you must know something about this guy Jesus. What were this guy's last words?"

He looked at me, kind of puzzled.

I said, "Our Lord said, 'Forgive them, Father, for they know not what they do.' I'm not going to go through life every time someone takes advantage of me just thinking they don't know what they did, but you know, it shouldn't change my attitude. I've got to be who I am. And who I am is being open and helpful. If you want to take advantage of that, then so be it."

So if I've given my name and phone number and e-mail and all that, then yeah, some people could abuse it probably. I've got a young lady I dated who thinks it's ridiculous that I do that. She said, "How could you open up to all these young people and give them your name and phone number?"

Well, what are they going to do with it? You know, I've just gotta think, what would they do with it? You have to have a few crazies along the twenty years I've been making speeches, but nothing that's going to harm me. I firmly believe you're going to take advantage only because you don't know what you're doing.

I had another night, by the way, helping a young man in Life's Directions, and a similar thing happened. We were at a party, and I grabbed this young man by the arm and said, "Merry Christmas."

He said, "Get your effin' arm off me."

"What do you mean?"

"I'm going to stab you. Get your hand off me."

I backed away, and I was just distraught. Now wait a minute, I just raised $250,000 to help kids like this in San Antonio, and here's this young man telling me he's going to stab me. And that's the first time I heard the Lord's words: "Forgive them, Father, for they know not what they do." And I had to believe that, because he didn't know what he was doing.

You know two weeks later that young man and I sat in my seats in Row 3 at a Spurs game. I brought him to the game. He looked at me and I said, "You didn't know what you were doing. You're okay, aren't you, George?" And we continued to communicate. Just because you gotta give them another chance. That's what I did. I gave him another chance.

I have heard Roy give the same speech countless times, and every time I hear it I come home motivated to make the most out of every minute that I have.

I use those five Fs of success on a daily basis and even have a tracking measure that I highly recommend. It is a very simple way to create a personal action plan that will make sure you are achieving success in each of the five Fs.

I have dry-erase boards in my home office that I use for everything from mapping out marketing plans to planning my day. Every Sunday evening I go to the whiteboard and write out:

FAMILY

FINANCES

FITNESS

FAITH

FUN

BLOG ME:
ypsuccess.com
What works
best for you?

I then reflect on the past week and I give each one a grade: A, B, C, D, or F. I use the plus and minus signs, too! So for example, this past week my wife and I spent some great quality time together; I talked to my grandmother on the phone a few times; enjoyed a beer with my dad on my back patio; and had a chance to talk to my sister. I didn't get a chance to check in on my mom, so it wasn't a perfect family week. So I wrote down an A-, because it was great, but not perfect.

Looking at finances, I thought that this past week we could have done a better job at watching the entertainment dollars we spent. So I gave a grade of B. And so on.

Now with a full set of grades, I look at them and say, "What can I do to get that grade to an A+?" For family, it was simple. I need to continue what I'm doing, but make sure I include my mom in the mix! For finances, my action item was to make sure that we did not eat out or go for drinks more than twice this week.

When you start grading yourself on a weekly basis, you become acutely aware of what you are doing well in your life and what can be improved. Also, by creating a list of small action items to get your grades to an A+, you give yourself a road map on how you can live your life in the best manner possible.

What are you grades this week? What can you do this week to get those grades to an A+? Try it out. You may surprise yourself—perhaps you are already doing well in some of the five Fs, and you may realize there is always room for improvement in our lives.

Linda Rimer
Senior Vice President, Asia/Pacific and Americas
JUNIOR ACHIEVEMENT WORLDWIDE

The best advice I could give to a young professional is this:

1. **Understand yourself**. Know what gives you energy and joy. Use your God-given talent in the line of work that you choose. When you are using your strengths and love what you do, you will do it well and get energy from it.
2. **Stand for what you believe**. Use your value system as an anchor. In life's ups and downs you must have an anchor to hold you firm in your foundation. Know what you stand for; if you don't stand for something, you will fall for anything. Make a list of the non-negotiables in your life. Integrity should be on everyone's list. Your character is built by the values that you will not compromise.
3. **Have your own measurement of success**. Do not measure by anyone else's standards. Salary, status, title, and prestige are

some measurements, but do not necessarily need to be yours. Yours may be joy, fulfillment, or making a difference in this world. Only you can determine the measurement. Set your own measurement of success as your goal.

If the five Fs system doesn't work for you, find another way to measure your success according to the values you hold dear. One way or another, be sure to analyze your goals according to what is truly important to you—not just according to the empty promises of "getting ahead" or reaching a certain monetary goal or status level. Seek out another method for making the intangible—your ethical standards, your happiness, your desire to make a difference—tangible in your life.

John F. Lundgren
Chairman & CEO
THE STANLEY WORKS

This is neither a story nor a quote, but hopefully some sound advice for young professionals in general and particularly those seeking career advancement and satisfaction in larger corporations.

Simply stated: It's a marathon, not a sprint.

Too many high-potential people forfeit successful careers because their ambitions get ahead of their capabilities or experience. One needs to set ambitious but reasonable career goals and personal milestones, and to ensure that he or she is learning every step of the way. Never become complacent or too comfortable in a particular role, but at the same time don't get wrapped around your own axle if a promotion or anticipated next step doesn't come as soon as you targeted or expected it.

If the organization is not growing or demonstrating reasonable growth prospects in the foreseeable future, it's probably best to apply your talents elsewhere. On the other hand, if growth prospects are evident but your learning curve is flattening out, be willing to accept or proactively seek lateral moves to expose you to different functions or environments that you can leverage within your existing organization—or ultimately the next one, if you conclude you are not in the right place.

Seek and demand feedback on performance, and look for arrows missing from the quiver that are keeping you from reaching the next level of increased responsibilities and, ultimately, increased rewards. Leverage your strengths, but focus on constructive criticism and areas of performance and behavior that need to be modified to achieve your ultimate goals. Your strengths alone may not get you where you want to go, but unaddressed weaknesses will almost certainly keep you from getting there.

> Don't let ambitions get ahead of capability or experience.

Jeffrey Berding
Director of Sales & Public Affairs
CINCINNATI BENGALS

My first job out of college was working for the Ohio attorney general on his campaign staff as he ran for governor.

My direct boss was Kevin, who had come into Ohio from Washington, D.C., where he directed a Senate committee for one of our Ohio senators. On a major campaign, working until nine, ten, or even midnight was common. You truly are giving your life for a time to the candidate.

I recall that every night before he left, Kevin would ask the campaign manager if he needed any help or whether there was more work for the night. Then, every morning when I got to the office, Kevin was always there. Maybe he was just reading the morning newspapers, but he was in the office. If I got in after nine a.m., as I walked by his office, he would say, with a bit of wit and sarcasm, "Good afternoon! Thanks for joining us today." It was just enough to make me feel a bit chagrined.

So when I was lying in bed, wanting to sleep a bit longer, I thought of Kevin's sarcastic greeting and got up. With that experience, I learned early in my professional life to always get to the office early, ahead of your boss, and never leave before asking your boss if there was more work to be done or assistance that could be provided to help him or her leave earlier.

It ended up working for me, as two years later, Kevin was named campaign manager for Senator John Glenn, and he hired me to be on his staff in the role he had served for the attorney general.

Some of the best advice I can give is to be a sponge. Absorb advice, seek it out, and learn from everyone you can. It is one of the reasons you are reading this book, and it's why these contributions from the CEOs and other leaders are so valuable. I probably go to more of an extreme with the Soak It Up concept than most do, but that's because learning from people, books, magazines, blogs, and other sources of information has been of extreme value in my career thus far.

I look at every interaction with someone as an opportunity to learn. Mostly, I love to find out what people do in their jobs. I don't ask the traditional "Hey, so what do you do for a living?" I ask a question that may take people off guard but gives me a better understanding of what they do. When a person tells me his title and who he works for, I ask the open-ended question "So, what does that mean you do during the day?"

At first the person usually looks at me funny, because it is not a question that is normally asked. But the answers can be fantastic!

"People love talking about themselves."

Some people get really excited when talking about their job and what they do on a day-to-day basis. A lot of the assumptions you make about certain occupations can be either erased or confirmed.

The art of learning from others provides a huge benefit to you. Not only do you gain knowledge, but you build a strong relationship with that person. You have probably heard this in every business book out there, but people love talking about themselves. I have yet to find someone who does not have at least one thing they are proud of or love to share. It may not be their job, but perhaps it's their kids, hobbies, or church. If you ask people questions and get them to talk about themselves, they actually view you as a more memorable person. Weird, right? When I was just getting started in business, I thought I had to tell everyone about myself to be memorable, but in fact, it's the other way around!

Randy Gordon
President & CEO
LONG BEACH AREA CHAMBER OF COMMERCE

One piece of advice I give young professionals just starting their careers is to spend the first year observing, listening, and asking questions.

The first year of a young professional's career lays the foundation for the years to come. It is true that today's young professionals, unlike those of generations before them (like me), will have numerous jobs in their career.

It is always the first job that sets the groundwork for future opportunities. Therefore, young professionals can secure a solid foundation and maximize the most opportunities early in their career by spending time learning from others around them. That learning can only be done by asking questions and listening to the answers, and then applying advice to exceed the expectations of the people around them.

> Spend the first year observing, listening, and asking questions.

There comes a time in a young professional's career when he or she will know the time is right to take a stand and do the talking. I can remember one particular young man I hired for a public policy job a few years ago, who really displayed great listening and learning skills and always seemed to know when to listen and when to speak. Today he is very successful, and I strongly believe that his success started in the beginning with his good use of these skills.

The art of listening and learning is not something that comes naturally to most people. You have to make an effort and be focused on it. One person comes to mind who seems to have mastered listening and learning to such a degree that it is entirely natural to him. It is no mystery why one of my mentors, General Bill J. Boles, became a four-star general in the United States Air Force.

When I first met General Boles, I noticed that he never seemed to misspeak. Everything he said was well calculated and thoughtful, and he always seemed to say the right thing at the right time. I started observing him to see what he did differently than everyone else.

First of all, General Boles never interrupts. It is not uncommon in most conversations, whether with business associates or with friends, for people to be so focused on saying what they want to say that they interrupt others. Subtle interruptions are accepted by most people as a normal part of communication—not so with an avid, accomplished listener.

General Boles also looks for clarity in a conversation. It is wise in business never to make assumptions, because you may be simply coming up with your own conclusion based on limited facts. In conversations with General Boles, you can expect clarifying questions. He never offers his own opinions or ideas without first getting all the information he needs—which is why every time he speaks, he never seems to make a mistake!

Finally, it is quite clear that he is constantly learning. By not interrupting and by asking clarifying questions, General Boles is always gathering new information, which also allows him to avoid the fatal flaw of making assumptions. This type of active listening can make all the difference, whether you see the results today or a sometime down the road.

Douglas S. Kinsinger
President & CEO
GREATER TOPEKA CHAMBER OF COMMERCE

Your local chamber of commerce provides a wonderful opportunity to learn, develop a career, or make contacts.

In 1979, as I attended the University of Northern Iowa, I had the opportunity to take an entry-level position as a college intern at the Waterloo, Iowa, Chamber of Commerce. The executive and volunteer leadership at the Waterloo chamber was excellent and provided me with an opportunity to learn from individuals whom I never would have met during my regular college curriculum.

As colleagues were promoted to management or left the Waterloo Chamber for another position, I asked for the opportunity to try to fulfill their responsibilities, offering to do so without asking for much more compensation. I learned much during these times. I tried to network and get involved in other parts of the organization, so I could learn as much as possible about chambers of commerce and the business world. I continued to work in a department management role, taking the collaborative responsibility for three previously separate positions.

I have now had the opportunity to be the president and CEO at five additional chamber organizations. Each organization has provided me the opportunity to work with some incredibly talented and skillful business executives, elected officials, and community leaders. Learning from my mistakes was probably the most difficult challenge to go through, but gaining the experience of how to handle the next similar situation differently was important.

I currently have the honor of serving as chairman of the board of the American Chamber of Commerce Executives, our national professional development association, which represents more than 8,500 other chamber professionals. I learned early on that I can learn something from every individual and that every day is an opportunity to learn, and I still live by those guidelines. By continuing to make myself a more capable and qualified leader and executive, I ultimately become more valuable to my employer and the community I serve.

My advice for young professionals is to recognize that your job is to learn as much as you can from a wide variety of sources. Individuals who possess a real hunger to learn will often realize that learning is a lifelong proposition that never ends. Your value to an organization is based upon the personal knowledge and skill you bring to that organization. In addition, organizations need leaders and seek out individuals who have had leadership experience and demonstrate leadership traits.

By interning or volunteering at your local chamber of commerce, you will have a unique opportunity to learn from some of your community's best and brightest business leaders, and to gain valuable leadership experience.

I am a huge fan of local chambers of commerce, so I thank Doug and all the chamber executives who contributed to this book.

However, let me caution you not to make the number one mistake of those who join their local chamber: do not expect the chamber to provide you leads, get you business, or automatically match you up with all the people you want to meet. You get out of the chamber what you give to the chamber. Do not ever be one of those new chamber members who does not volunteer for a committee or build a network wisely, and who then says, "I got nothing out of the chamber. One year, and not a single business deal." Get involved, and ask those who have been involved what they have done to make the most of their membership. And when you're listening to the answer, remember: don't interrupt, and ask questions to clarify!

In sales, the importance of "pre-call planning" is stressed over and over again. Pre-call planning is ensuring that before you walk in the door to meet with a prospect, you have established clearly defined goals and objectives. It sounds like a no-brainer, but all too often, pre-call planning does not occur. I sometimes make up to ten sales calls in a day, and it is important to walk into each office with a clear objective. The results are obvious to me; when I have established a clear, concise objective, my success rate with a prospect is much higher.

> "*When you're listening to the answer, remember: don't interrupt, and ask questions to clarify.*"

Pre-call planning does not just apply to sales, however. Always prepare goals and objectives for anything that has to do with business. As Essie Calhoun, chief diversity officer of Eastman Kodak Company, says, we all have a personal brand that we need to manage. Every word you say is advertising for your personal brand. It could be good advertising or it could be bad advertising. This is especially true in the case of first impressions—you will never get the opportunity for a second one.

If you are entering an office for the first time for any business purpose, follow these simple pre-call planning steps:

1. Observe the office space.
2. Repeat everyone's name that you meet until it sticks
3. Find out what each person in the organization does.

Listen. Don't Interrupt. Clarify. That's it. It is that simple.

You have limited time every day, so gain knowledge from every interaction. The only way to do that is to prepare yourself with pre-call planning for every interaction you have.

Essie L. Calhoun
Chief Diversity Officer & Director of Community Affairs
EASTMAN KODAK COMPANY

During my career, I have held a number of different positions. I began as a teacher, earned a master's degree, became a school administrator, and then switched my career to business. I became a sales representative for Kodak, moved into a marketing position, and then moved into a role in public affairs.

Manage your brand: YOU.

Today, I wear two hats—chief diversity officer and director of community affairs. And I borrow a little experience from each of my previous assignments to do my current job.

Making the leap from education to business wasn't easy. But it became possible when I stepped back and asked myself, "What else can I do with my education?" Which of my skills were transferable to the business world? What skills were transferable into what roles?

Young men and women beginning their careers must be willing to keep an open mind. Given today's pace of change, the career they train for as undergraduates may evolve just a few years after they graduate. That is why I urge young people to develop a broad range of competencies, and to look for opportunities to apply their skills in other ways.

One of the most important assets to a company is its brand, so much so that we have whole departments focused on brand management and senior executives with titles like chief marketing officer. The CMO is not responsible just for marketing the company, but also for managing the brand.

You, too, have a brand to manage. That brand is you. It has always been important to me to manage my brand. You need to identify your own personal brand attributes. So ask yourself: Who am I? What do I stand for? What do others think of me as a person? As a colleague? A friend? A leader? A businessperson?

Aside from learning from people, I also want to mention the wealth of information that can be soaked up from magazines, blogs, and books. Other than the Internet, magazines are probably the least expensive source of information. I subscribe to many business magazines, including *Inc.*, *Fast Company*, *Entrepreneur*, *Forbes*, and *Fortune*. Most have a price tag of only $10–$20 per year—a small price to pay for an incredible amount of excellent information. I highly recommend finding some trade magazines that fit your interests (marketing, design, engineering, etc.) and subscribing to them right away. If you want a little more in-depth business reading, I highly recommend the *Harvard Business Review*; at about $100 per year, it is more expensive but well worth the price.

Even though most business leaders might say that business books are more valuable than business magazines, I recommend trying out a magazine subscription before diving into a business book club commitment. It's not just the low-end monetary investment; another great thing about a magazine subscription is that it makes for a quick read. You can pick up the magazine, read one or two articles that are of interest to you, and just thumb through the rest. This means that magazines are an extremely appropriate vehicle for members of Generation A.D.D. Not to mention that a monthly publication is always up to date!

My favorite magazine, *Inc.*, has a lot of one- or two-page articles that are perfect for my short attention span. Go to your nearest library or bookstore and simply skim the titles and bylines to see which articles appeal to you and which do not—and then decide which publications are worth your dime. There are also many magazines you can receive for free. Check out magazines.com for a huge selection of freebies and paid-subscription options.

Check out *www.magazines.com* for free mags

As far as books go, I do recommend reading them—naturally! I am an avid reader and have become a business book addict in the past few years. My mother-in-law keeps checking for reassurance from my wife: "Does he really just want books for Christmas?" She assumes that the books she buys (with advice from my wife) are for work and not for fun. As it turns out, while this may seem like a scary thought, business books are fun for me, too. The trick is figuring out exactly what type of business books you like. Being in marketing and sales, of course, I favor marketing and sales books. I usually can gain some new idea or a concept that applies to my own work. I also find myself gravitating to books on leadership and organizational culture. With most of us spending more time at work than we do with our families, these books can provide superior value in terms of making your work environment more enjoyable and productive.

Think about what topics interest you. Don't read a business book just because it is on the bestseller list. The best way to find quality books is through other people. When you find yourself at your first chamber of commerce event, here is a great question to ask: "Have you read a good book recently on leadership (or whatever topic interests you)?"

James L. Wainscott
Chairman, President & CEO
AK STEEL CORPORATION

Leadership is a great privilege, but you have to be ready to lead. When I was named president and CEO of AK Steel in the fall of 2003, my father-in-law, a blue-collar worker from Pittsburgh and one of the world's greatest guys, asked me, "Now that you are CEO, who's going to tell you what to do?" My reply was simply this: "If I don't know what to do by now, I'm in trouble and so is this company."

I am not sure that anyone can ever be completely ready to run a Fortune 500 company, but it certainly helps if you have some experience at managing departments or divisions. I was fortunate to have had that experience and to have paid more than twenty years of so-called "dues" in the steel business. No one likes to be told that he or she needs to gain experience and "pay their dues," but I can assure you that it is good advice.

Jim recommends *What Really Matters,* by John Pepper

If you are fortunate, as I have been, to make it to the top, it is essential that you know your business—your people, your customers and markets, your products, and your competition. Candidly assess your company's strengths and weaknesses. Mostly, you need to know how and where your company makes its money—and where it is losing money.

Even with the greatest of educations, there is simply no substitute for experience. Be a sponge for knowledge. Learn everything you can about the company and the industry, because when you are the president and CEO of a company, you are expected to know these things…or else.

Being ambitious is an admirable quality, but there is simply no substitute for the time and effort it takes on your part to get ahead. While it's true you are accountable to your board of directors and shareholders, ultimately, you are accountable to yourself.

So make sure you are ready to tell yourself what to do in case you get the opportunity to lead. And be sure to make your father-in-law proud.

Blogs, which I mentioned above, are the newest and most accessible source of "soakable" information about your career interests, whatever they may be. As with books, there are thousands and thousands of blogs about different topics and of varying quality. I make it part of my morning routine to read both a local and a national newspaper online, and then read my specified blogs—before I allow myself to catch up on my sports news at ESPN.com.

I am fairly new to the blogging and social media world (find me at ypsuccess.com or through Twitter at twitter.com/ryankohnen), so I am hardly qualified to be your expert resource on blogs. For that I called on the greatest resource I've met regarding technology, information, and communication: Nan Palmero, chief inspiration officer of Sales By 5. Learn from his practical advice below, and then check out the blog to which Nan contributes regularly at salesby5.com.

twitter me
ryankohnen

Nan Palmero
Chief Inspiration Officer
SALES BY 5

twitter me
nanpalmero

What value can you get out of blogs?

Historically, the newest information about our industry (sales and marketing) has come from textbooks, trade publications, journals, and traditional websites. Now, blogs have come into the picture as an addition to these valuable resources. Great blogs are updated anywhere from several times a day to once a week. The speed and quality of the postings can provide you with the latest information available in your industry. Now you no longer need to wait for monthly updates.

Consider how difficult it is for someone who reads magazines and journals to compete against you, receiving daily updates. Although it may seem as if receiving these blogs is an overload of information, it is actually the opposite. You save time by reading blogs because the content has been tailored specifically to a certain topic, so you read only what you are seeking and nothing more. Some blogs provide a superior global picture with posts from other countries, as it may be difficult otherwise to find information from those countries. Other blogs scour the media wires and provide updates of new technology, processes, or offerings from companies. You might even find some bloggers writing about product leaks and breaking news before the mainstream media is able to report on these things. The speed at which a blog is able to provide information is far superior to most competing venues of communication.

How can you find blogs that are pertinent to your interests?

Whether you are in a specialized industry of, say, plastics moldings or in something more traditional such as managing sales, there is likely a blog out there for you. Sometimes, however, it can be difficult to find a good blog for your industry. The easiest way to find one is to do a Google search; it's as easy as typing marketing blog or plastics blog. Once you've found some blogs, you can skim through them and see if the information is of value to you.

Nan recommends *The Truth About You,* by Marcus Buckingham

If you'd prefer to take someone else's word for which blogs are great, you can do that, too! Try posting a question on a social networking site, such as LinkedIn or Facebook. A simple question such as "Can anyone recommend a great PR blog?" can yield numerous results within a few hours.

Another opportunity is to check out blog ranking sites, where blogs earn their reputation by the number of times they are quoted by other sites. One example is technorati.com, which displays "Authority" (credibility based on previously determined criteria) and lists inbound links to each particular blog.

What tools are there to manage blogs?

There is a never-ending list of available resources to manage your blog subscriptions. Every day there are new ways to consume your content, depending upon your hardware device or the way you'd like to receive the information. You can always access blogs by going directly to the Web address, but this is the least efficient way to view the information.

The preferred means of reading blogs is through an RSS reader or feed reader. RSS ("really simple syndication") shortens the time you spend looking for new content from your preferred blogs. Your RSS reader updates you instead of you having to search for new content.

As Lee and Sachi LeFever of Common Craft so eloquently explain (http://www.commoncraft.com/rss_plain_english), RSS is similar in nature to Netflix. You select the specific items that you would like to review, and you're sent only those items. You don't have to go out to get the information; instead, the information comes to you. This reduces the clutter that you have to process.

Now that you understand the value of RSS readers, you are probably eager to know which ones to use. One of the most popular desktop methods is Google Reader (www.google.com/reader), which allows you to search for new feeds directly, through a Google search bar, and subscribe to them in just a few steps. Or you can simply search for a keyword, such as marketing and get some of the popular feeds. Once you have found great feeds—and more important, a great article—you have various options. You can star an article for future review or share it with your other Google Reader friends.

A second choice is reading blogs via your browser. Using a browser such as Firefox, you can view these feeds directly or through the use of Firefox extensions. Another great option is to use your e-mail program, such as Outlook or Entourage, to receive your feeds. If you are on the go and have a smartphone, check out Viigo (www.getviigo.com). Viigo allows you to maintain synchronization with Google Reader on your desktop, so you don't have to reenter your feeds on your mobile device. If you choose to read feeds strictly on your smart phone, you can manage your list of feeds through your phone or through Viigo's portal (www.myviigo.com). If you find an article that you'd like to save, Viigo provides you the option of e-mailing the article to yourself or to someone else, saving the article, or posting it to Delicious (www.delicious.com). These options allow you to maintain a virtual library of information that you can use at a later date.

I must thank Nan for hooking me up with Viigo, and I highly recommend that application for your smartphone. My advice is to always be open to the latest opportunity to connect with others who share your interests. Who knows what information network might be coming down the pike?

FIND MENTORS AND CREATE FANS

Find mentors, give and receive value, and then come full circle back to being a mentor yourself.

8

The concept of Finding Mentors and Creating Fans is truly just an extension of the principles of Soak It Up, but it relies specifically on a type of continuous learning: the mentor relationship.

I have yet to meet someone who has achieved remarkable success who doesn't say how instrumental his or her mentors were along the journey to the top. Mentors can be parents, your first boss, friends, business partners, spouses, a pastor, or almost anyone else with whom you interact. They typically have one thing in common: mentors have "been there and done that," so their advice and knowledge can be invaluable.

Most people have mentors in their lives, but you may have not made that association or referred to these people as such. Do you have someone in your life whom you bounce ideas off regarding your career or your current job? Is there someone you turn to when you are in a bind? These people are your mentors. You do not have to have just one. You may have many mentors, and they can be a great source of help and inspiration.

The benefits of having mentors are numerous. Those I have had in my life have helped me with everything from career direction to balancing my work and personal lives. My mentors have given me advice on continuing my education, have assessed my strengths and weaknesses, have provided a neutral opinion when I am involved in a conflict. In the chapter "It's Not What You Know…," I talk about the importance of building your network of people. Mentors can be a huge asset in building that network.

The current chapter includes information on how to find great mentors, how to best make use of them, how to avoid dangerous mentors, how to give back to your mentors, and finally, how to become a mentor yourself.

While many people might suggest finding an "official" mentor, I do not have one, and I dispense with the formality of actually asking someone to be my mentor. Instead I use a process of creating "mini-mentors."

It works like this: At another one of my sales conferences, there was one sales manager I noticed in particular. He happened to be sitting next to me at this conference, and I took the opportunity to get to know him and learn how he became a sales manager. I found out that we had a similar background and a similar business philosophy. He was about ten years older than me, had more experience than me, and was also a previous business owner. I realized that this was an opportunity to learn!

Because he lived about 1,500 miles away, this gentleman would not have been an ideal candidate for a traditional mentor, but you can bet I added him to my mini-mentor list. I meet mini-mentors all the time, and in all likelihood so do you—they're those people from whom you can learn something in any conversation by just paying attention to their experiences and knowledge. Mini-mentors may not be people with whom I interact on a weekly or monthly basis, but I have called on this particular sales manager twice throughout the past year when I've felt that his background and experiences would apply to a specific problem or question that I have.

So I advise you to look at everyone as a potential mini-mentor. You will also build relationships faster and more successfully when you treat someone as a mentor, instead of treating them simply as a friend. You'll impress them just by wanting to learn from them. Don't believe me? Ask Dave Habiger.

Dave Habiger
President & CEO
SONIC SOLUTIONS

Be optimistic, smile, and demonstrate your desire to work hard.

Intelligence matters, but not as much as hard work and experience. Most important, keep striving to find the job that you absolutely love; at the very least, you will find something you like.

At age twenty-four, I was responsible for managing the Pacific Rim region and building a dealer channel there for my company's products. When doing business in Japan and China, cultures where age really matters, I was always the youngest guy in the room. I learned that the senior executives I dealt with, all of them age fifty-plus, initially had little respect for me, given my age and lack of experience.

It was only when I asked them to help guide me so I could learn from them that they transformed into great supporters and advocates. They wanted to see me succeed, and they rooted for me in the same way a parent wants their kids to succeed.

Trying to prove I was just as knowledgeable and experienced as they were, which I was not, would have only provoked the opposite response.

> Intelligence matters, but not as much as hard work and experience.

Mini-mentors are those individuals whom you run into on a daily basis in your normal job and life, and from whom you pick up bits of helpful advice here and there. However, true mentors are harder to find, and it takes more work to nurture this sort of relationship.

When I look for mentors, I try to find people who have accomplished what I would like to accomplish in the future. If I meet someone who appears to love his job, who has a great family life, and who makes a significant impact on the community, I know this is a person I want to learn from and know. He may have a different personality or background, but he is experiencing the success that I would like to achieve.

By putting yourself in the right environment, you may meet potential mentors while carrying out your daily activities. I attend a lot of business conferences and charity events, and I'm involved in a number of nonprofit organizations. Through these interactions, I meet many new people on a weekly basis.

If you are more of a nine-to-five employee with little contacts other than meeting your friends at a local pub, you may have to develop more of a strategy in order to seek out and find a mentor than would someone who has built-in networking opportunities. So how do you accomplish this? First, you may try expanding your horizons and venturing to business conferences, industry association events, or charity occasions. You can also look to online communities, your parents' friends, local business owners, or the person you just met on a plane ride back to your hometown.

"Never think in terms of 'I need a good mentor,' but instead, 'I need many good mentors.'"

Never think in terms of "I need a good mentor," but instead, "I need many good mentors." I have different mentors for different aspects of my life. Some people I recognize as leadership mentors, who teach and advise me on key leadership decisions. I also have mentors who guide me in my educational development or my personal life or my marketing strategies in particular. I look for mentors from a diverse group of people with different backgrounds and experiences.

Many potential mentors are likely to exist within your own organization. There are certainly opportunities here, but I suggest looking outside your current organization to avoid any possibility of a conflict of interest. The most important aspect of a mentor-mentee relationship is honesty, and it may be challenging to be completely honest when what is bothering you may be that person or the organization itself. A manager to whom you report directly is definitely someone you can learn from and who could be an advocate for you, but it may not be a good idea to have that person as one of your mentors.

Luckily, potential mentors are everywhere. When you meet someone who you feel could be your mentor, you can take two approaches. First, trust your instincts and your observations about human behavior; allow these to help you determine whether the person you are approaching is willing to consider a mentoring relationship. If you are unsure of the potential mentor's interest, then ask! A simple, straightforward question should suffice: "I am impressed with the way you lead your organization and balance your family life. Would you mind if I called on you if I am seeking advice or help in my efforts in doing the same?"

However you establish a mentor relationship, it is important to outline expectations when you approach a possible mentor. There is also a fine line between being considerate of your mentor and bothering him or her by taking up too much valuable time. If you are expecting this person to go to lunch with you monthly or be able to answer your phone calls in the evening, you must reveal that expectation up front and ask if that is alright with him or her. Some such privileges may be earned only through the furthering of the relationship, but whatever your initial expectations are, make sure your mentor is in agreement.

Roy H. Williams
President & CEO
GREATER OKLAHOMA CITY CHAMBER OF COMMERCE

As a young professional in the field of my choice, I was very hungry—not just for furthering my academic knowledge, but also for understanding the application and implementation of my knowledge.

To that end I was very careful in selecting a mentor whom I could call, counsel with, and ask questions of, and from whom I could generally get perspectives I did not have. I was careful not to overburden that person, yet I made sure that we had an agreement so I could basically call at will. As I grew up in my profession, I developed many mini-mentors whom I engaged frequently. My philosophy was, if I wanted to be successful in my profession, then I had to look like a professional, act like a professional, and do what professionals did—only better.

In essence, I picked many of the individual best traits from the best professionals and built on them.

So now you have found a person on whom you would like to model your career, and you have outlined the expectations for your relationship and determined a suitable manner of communicating. Perhaps you have agreed to meet quarterly for lunch, and your mentor has encouraged you to call at other times if you need some advice or assistance with a decision.

Your first goal in your mentoring relationship is to define what you want to achieve through the relationship—your goals of learning. For example, if you sought out a mentor based on his or her career progression within a corporate environment, keep your focus on your career progression in your own organization. Maintaining a specific focus will allow you to get into detail and be open and honest with your mentor.

One big mistake I made when I first had mentors was contacting them only when I was seeking approval. When I had an idea about something for my personal life or in terms of business, I wanted to hear what a great idea it was. I needed positive reinforcement. It was not until I truly listened and tried to learn from the mentor that I received the most value from the relationship. The best mentors ask great questions. They do not tell you what to do, but instead they coach and challenge you to make your own

> *"The best mentors ask great questions."*

decisions. Good mentors offer their own experiences and challenge your viewpoints. Sometimes what they say may hurt, but constructive criticism is often the most helpful feedback. Your only expectation from your mentors should be complete honesty. And sometimes you will also get that positive reinforcement.

Bart Childers
President
TMS COMPUTER SERVICES

Sometimes life is funny: you have lots of advice to give, but is anyone listening? Anyway, here goes (from William Shakespeare): "To thine own self be true, and it must follow, as the night the day, thou canst not then be false to any man."

How do you apply that to business and life? It sounds simple, but in reality it is very hard to do. Many people lead double lives, one person at home and another, dissatisfied person at work. They take jobs that they are not suited for, because of the pressure for success or money. They while away their time at that job or similar jobs, because the job chose them. Everyone tells them that this is okay—it's normal.

How do you want to be remembered?

I know, this is a little on the dark side. But it doesn't have to be this way. Remember the thoughts you had as a kid? The things that you wanted to be or that you wanted to do? Try to think back to that, and then focus on today: how do you want to be remembered?

Learn to really know yourself—meaning what you can and cannot do well, what fits you, and what you like. Only then can you make a choice about what you really want to do with your life. You will feel pressure from everyone else to become something that they feel is defined as "successful." Some people will tell you, "Save some money, then save the world." In life, though, you will be the one who has to account for your decision.

If you see yourself as a leader and ruler, then you must do things that warrant you being in charge and leading others.

Thanks, Bart, for being a mentor of mine—and yes, we are listening! How do I make sure that I'm putting my all into my work—and getting the most value out of it? What do I want to accomplish in the long run? These are the sort of "big picture" questions that a mentor can help a young professional remember to ask…and answer.

Richard W. (Rick) Frost
Chief Executive Officer
LP BUILDING PRODUCTS
(formerly Louisiana-Pacific Corporation)

My boss, the division president, called me at 6:00 a.m., gave me a cup of coffee, and said he had a project for me.

We had a mill losing upwards of $300,000 per month. He wanted me, as his staff guy, to go to the mill and turn it around. The rules were 1) You can't fire the manager; 2) You can't spend any capital; 3) You have ninety days. I asked him when he wanted me to get started. His only response was to look at his watch—which meant "right now." This was his normal M.O.

I went home, packed, and was on a plane by noon. By working two of the three shifts for about eighty days—that's fifteen hours a day, seven days a week—I helped pare the losses to less than $75,000 per month. Much better, but still not the desired result.

After the ninety days ran out, the division president called me on a Friday and told me to come home and meet with him and the CEO.

After listening to my story, the CEO said, "I hate to put you in this position, but if you were me, what would you do?"

I stated that within the rules I had been given by my boss, I could do no more. The only answer was to close the location. The CEO responded that we were to do so that afternoon, and in fact we were to use the corporate aircraft to complete the task that very day.

By 4:00 p.m., we had finished the deed and I was driving my president back to the airport in a very depressed and somber state. After about thirty minutes of silence, my boss said, "Frost, what's the matter?" I responded, "Well, two things. First, we just fired 130 really good people whom I have worked beside for three months. Second, this was the first thing that you have ever asked me to do that I could not get done for you."

Without pause, he smiled and said, "Heck, Frost, I know you couldn't accomplish that task when I sent you down here, but I needed to do two things. First, these are good people, and I had to assure myself that closure was the only solution. Second, I wanted to teach you an invaluable lesson."

I went ballistic. I cursed him every which way from Sunday. I went on and on about how hard I had worked, the hours I put in, the three months I had spent away from my wife and my small children.

I finally stopped, as he was still grinning at me, and I inquired, "Just what is this darned lesson that I was supposed to learn that was this important?"

He said, "First, as you become more powerful, you need to remember that the decisions you make affect real people and their families. When management fails, good people, other than management, suffer. Second, you needed to learn something now, that will save you and your future employees millions of dollars later—that is, that sometimes, no matter how hard you try or how hard you work, you just can't fix some things—because you either run out of time or you run out of money—or both."

> "*When management fails, good people, other than management, suffer.*"

He went on to bet me $10 that within ten years I would catch myself teaching some other, younger manager the same lesson.

I sent him his $10 after only five years.

* * * * * * * * * *

I got out of high school at seventeen and went offshore as a janitor on the oil rigs. My first job in my current industry was as a forester and logger. Today, I am CEO of a large public forest industries company—

a very unlikely career path. It has given me some interesting experiences, some of which have left me with good advice to pass along.

1. Learn to communicate through stories, metaphors, and analogies. People remember them.
2. Read, read, read—with an insatiable appetite. Read everything you can get your hands on. Two years before I became CEO, I decided to read the biographies of all the U.S. presidents in order to get ready for the job. I completed the task and what I learned has been invaluable to me.
3. To be an effective leader, you must develop and learn to articulate your value system. You need to know who you are and what you are willing to lose your job over.
4. Ethics and integrity are quite simply everything—and you must role model them above all else.
5. If you just want to work hard and you are totally honest, you will end up in the top 10 percent—I don't know who said this, but it is true.

One final contribution I would like to make is a quote (I do not know the source):

Be mindful of your thoughts, for they become your words.
Be choiceful of your words, for they become your actions.
Be purposeful in your actions, for they become your reputation.
Be protective of your reputation, for it becomes your legacy.

A word of caution when seeking mentors and beginning to build your relationship: make sure that there are not any potential ulterior motives or conflicts of interest. When I had my Web business, I sought out a professor of mine who also owned a technology and software business. He was brash and often bragged about his success, but I admired his intelligence and thought he could be a potential mentor for me. Since he was a professor, I assumed he had only my best interests at heart, and I placed my trust in him. (There is that word "assumption" again. Nothing good happens when you assume something.)

We met for lunch one day and were talking about the possibility of my business growing faster, although cash could be a potential problem because of equipment and software costs. This is when he offered to invest in my company. The offer sounded great. No one had ever proposed investing before, and I naively saw it as a simple case of giving me money for my business. The professor was willing to invest based on my needs; in return he would get partial ownership of my business. He encouraged me, saying that this would be great for me and my business and that if I wanted to grow, I needed to take on investors.

Luckily, I had another mentor, and I ran the idea by him. At the time, as I mentioned, I was just looking for positive reinforcement, because I was sold on the idea and wanted to move forward. But when the second mentor began asking questions, it became apparent that I did not need the money and that the only person who would gain from this arrangement was the professor.

In an almost ten-year career, I have only experienced this one potentially problematic situation, and I refer to it as a warning. It is very easy to trust someone whom you have sought out as a mentor. This is why it is best to foster more than one mentoring relationship; you'll always have great advice from multiple perspectives to steer you in the right direction.

Bryan S. Derreberry
President & CEO
WICHITA METRO CHAMBER OF COMMERCE

One of my mentors as a young professional state lobbyist for the Greater Cincinnati Chamber of Commerce was Senior Vice President Jim Wuenker. His professional specialty was economic development, but he really excelled in understanding and relating to human beings.

My favorite place to watch Jim and learn from him was in complex meetings. Jim would consistently sit back and watch the ebb and flow of a meeting and make an occasional comment or suggestion. He would conscientiously jot down a few critical points during the course of the meeting, just biding his time until the last few minutes.

Inevitably, as the meeting was winding down to its last ten or fifteen minutes, Jim would eloquently speak up and present a balanced solution that incorporated the best approaches that had been offered during the meeting, with a tone and slant that were advantageous to the Cincinnati chamber. All involved parties would be honored, the solution would generally be right on, and everyone would leave the meeting with a desire to implement the proposed outcome. I had to watch this multiple times to see how brilliant it was.

Jim did not have to hear himself talk, he did not have to fight for his position, there was no need to show how smart he was, and he did not get upset when things were not going his way. He did not have to win or show he was right—he simply exercised the patience and intellectual capacity to masterfully build and present solutions that everyone would agree to implement. I work hard to use and hone the same meeting leadership characteristics to this day. Any young

> Leaders who have little to say end up leading the pack.

professional would greatly benefit from walking this walk and studying leaders who say little but end up leading the whole pack.

The second thing I would offer to young professionals—and mine who do this are stars—is to accept full and complete ownership of whatever portion of the business you have been entrusted with. Run that piece of the business as though your livelihood depended on it, because ultimately it does. Have fun with your piece of business, be entrepreneurial, and use it to change how the customer perceives your overall business in a positive light. At four points during the year, report in to your supervisor on how your piece of the business is doing and the plans you have for it over the next two quarters.

It is amazing what happens when you own your part of the business versus just working at a place of business or working for someone. Try it and live it fully, and you will someday be running your own business or leading a company. I guarantee it!

Even mentors have mentors. So as you prepare to build a group of first-class mentors, consider becoming a mentor yourself.

If you are in the latter part of your "young" career, why not mentor someone recently out of college? If you are an out-of-college professional, why not mentor those who are currently in college? One of the best ways to help others—and yourself, while you're at it—is to bring an understanding of what it's like on the other side of the table.

Erik Darmstetter
Chief Energy Officer
SALES BY 5

twitter me
erikdarm

My first real business venture was in high school. I took pictures of football players and dance team girls and then sold them to one group or the other. A year out of high school, I went to Dallas Market Center and bought Jams—board shorts from the '80s—wholesale and sold them to friends and others.

Early in college, my fraternity had the ugliest shirts on campus, so I started designing and had much better-looking shirts printed. This started a path that has continued and developed throughout my life: I look at an existing problem, for myself and others, and find a solution that sells. I followed my heart to decide which designs to print, and eventually the shirts sold in retail stores nationally.

> Erik recommends *Fortune Small Business* magazine

Today, to make decisions, take on risk, or move forward in my life, I use these strong business tools I have been fortunate enough to learn:

1. **Following my heart**. Your intuition—your "gut feeling"—is sometimes hidden by opportunity or excitement. Every day, whether it's a decision in a meeting, a risk in taking on a new project or client, or a step in building a new relationship, something comes up that demands that I follow my heart. I have learned that it is okay to say no and to let others say no—not because their business is unwelcome, but because it wasn't the right fit. I have also learned to say yes when my heart is in it, even if risk is involved.

2. **Using my strengths**. I've learned about strengths and how they can completely change your life. What is a strength? An activity that you look forward to doing; an activity that make time fly; an activity where you feel in control. What is a weakness? An activity that makes you feel drained; an activity that makes you feel bored; an activity that you may be good at but that leaves you feeling unfulfilled. The key is applying your strengths a little more each day to truly feel and live a greater sense of fulfillment.

3. **Having standards**. There is acceptable and there is unacceptable. If I accept anything that I deem unacceptable, I have made it acceptable to me. I determine what is acceptable and unacceptable in my life and business—from people's attitudes to their behaviors to their methods of communication. I have learned that it rests on my shoulders to set the standard, reward the acceptable, and reject the unacceptable.

By using these elements, I have built a business full of clients, a business that my team believes in. Our hearts are in every project to which we give our time. I have created a positive and energetic work environment where we all encourage one another to use our strengths. This has created a team of challenged and fulfilled individuals who work together. I have stayed away from negative people and anyone who has told me I could not do something. I had "friends" in high school who constantly discouraged me; I was forced to make the difficult decision to keep them out of my life. The people in my life whom I want to be around are the ones who see my strengths and let me use them; they see my weaknesses and help me navigate around them.

> "Your 'gut feeling' is sometimes hidden by opportunity or excitement."

When I look back at the times when I had the most success, I was doing things for other people to give them either the benefit of a smile, pride in their personal brand, or a dramatic difference from their competitor. It was not about me! Finding out how to benefit other people has always been the most rewarding thing in my life, and has become my greatest purpose.

My mentors have done a lot of good things for me in my career. They have helped out on tough decisions or have gotten me to ask the tough questions. However, something that I did not anticipate was my mentors becoming friends, supporters, and fans of mine. They began to sing my praises to others and be champions for my goals and causes. This is an unexpected benefit of having a great relationship with your mentors. Your mentors will want you to succeed. By showing them your value, you can make them your biggest fans in the community.

So go out and find yourself some mentors. Learn from them and show gratitude; then come full circle and give your own time as a mentor. You will be learning, giving back, and creating fans throughout the process.

Jennifer Kohnen Kirsch
Marketing Professional

One Career Killer I witnessed was on the second day of this young man's first real job. He decided that the chair the company had given him in his cubicle was not what he wanted. Rather than "bother" anyone about it, he took matters into his own hands: he walked into the chief procurement officer's board room and replaced his chair with one of the nicer chairs in there. When his peer colleagues came around and saw that he had a new chair, they questioned it, and some advised him to put it back, realizing that it was not appropriate. It was not long before this was brought to the attention of the chief procurement officer. Unfortunately, from then on, this worker was viewed as lacking social graces. Who knows what damage this did to his budding career?

Rusty Rueff

Former CEO, SNOCAP INC.
Former Executive Vice President, ELECTRONIC ARTS INC.

Those at the top of today's organizations will all tell you that sometime early in their career they were given the opportunity to do something that they were neither chronologically or experientially ready to do. They were asked to jump into the deep end of the pool because they had proven up to that point that, when given a challenge, they delivered and even went further by going "the extra mile." When given the chance to take on the big challenge, successful people stepped up, and even though they might have bobbed up and down in the deep end, they kept their head above water. And then, just as important, they were humbled by that experience and learned what they didn't know, and through this they found ways to stay humble. Those who carried that experience and those lessons with them are the ones who get to the top fastest.

> Always go the extra mile, deliver more than asked, sooner than required.

The best tip I can give you about managing your boss is to always go the extra mile and deliver more than asked, sooner than required. When you do that, you take away all possible responses from your boss other than "Thank you."

My wife, Lacey, and I were enjoying a nice meal one evening with our friends Megan and Jacob Kluger. I met Jacob when I was running my Web development business and he was a partner in a

technology and start-up consulting firm. As fellow young entre-
preneurs with high energy and hopes, we became friends. Both
of us had been fortunate to achieve some success at an early age.
In addition, Megan and Lacey were also experiencing success and
happiness in their careers.

The previous chapter discussed the value in asking questions and learning from others. Megan had this art perfected,
as she showed us that evening with the following question: "We
have all seen success at a young age. To what do each of you
attribute this?"

What a great issue for discussion! We racked our brains. It
was interesting: the things that went through my head were my
failures. I realized that I have tried so many things and taken so
many risks, I feel prepared to handle a variety of situations. The
unique part is that most of my failures were intertwined with success, but it was the failing part of the project or venture that proved
to be the key learning experience.

Jacob mentioned the same thing. He, too, is adventurous and
risky, and he found that his mistakes and experiences were of the
most value to his career.

However, when Megan pushed us to think of what we had
done "right," we all agreed that it was our ability to build, nurture,
and maintain relationships with people. This is such a key point in
developing a young professional's career that a whole upcoming
chapter is devoted to it ("It's Not What You Know...").

Megan did get me thinking. What were the best mistakes that
I made? It sounds strange to actually think of my "best" mistakes,
but truthfully some mistakes are helpful and can change one's
life for the better. I would not be who I am today without going
through them.

Ellen J. Kullman
President & CEO
DUPONT

Throughout our lives we encounter events and opportunities that change our direction in ways we might never have anticipated. This is certainly true when it comes to our work life. There are two pieces of advice I would have for young people as they develop their careers. The first is to be open to new opportunities—even if you are happy with what you are doing—and the second is to be ready when an opportunity presents itself.

Young people today are being told that they could change careers three to five times during their lifetime and that they could have up to six jobs changes within a career. That's a lot of opportunity for career decision making.

I entered college knowing that I wanted to be an engineer, and I left with a degree in mechanical engineering. While that training still has value in what I do, I changed directions largely due to an opportunity I would not have anticipated.

During my first job after college, I accepted an opportunity to work in a sales position. To my surprise, I loved it. I really enjoyed the direct interaction with customers, and I learned that I was good at it. The results of this experience were a decision to pursue an MBA and a serious interest in becoming more involved with marketing and with building market-facing businesses.

I have learned to be ready for the opportunities to come. This means being aware of what is happening within our companies, so we can anticipate or respond to opportunities or needs. It means committing ourselves to being lifelong learners, so we have the skills and knowledge that will give us options. And it means being willing to take a risk, accepting that if we do not succeed, we will learn and benefit and grow from the experience.

GREAT MISTAKE #1: BEING TOO PROUD TO ASK FOR HELP

I was nineteen when I founded SA Web Tech, which later became Sawt, Inc. I had been buying and selling sports trading cards and memorabilia through eBay to make spending money while in college. Having built up a consistent client base, I thought it would be beneficial to set up my own website to sell my merchandise so that I could bypass the eBay commission.

So I took some of the money I had made from eBay, along with all my high school graduation money, and set out to build my sports memorabilia and trading card website. Over $1,000 later I was out of money and without a website. Now let me say that $1,000 is a lot of money to me today, but nothing like the amount of money it was when I was nineteen years old!

In 1999, the website development industry was a mess. It was a fairly new industry, so the Web designers and developers themselves—and not their clients—dictated how things were run. The average business owner that I met in San Antonio at this time was a fifty-year-old male. These business owners did not grow up with the Internet, nor did they have a grasp of Web design and development. This led to many stories like my own, with Web designers coming in with their T-shirts and flip-flops, throwing fancy technological verbiage in our direction, and leaving us without money and in a state of confusion as to how it all happened.

Out of frustration, I set out to build my own Web design and development company specifically for the fifty-year-old business owner who needed a little more guidance—who needed a "translator" for all the techno-jargon.

I found two extremely talented Web designers, Leslie Benito and Jason Tudor, and asked if they would be interested in doing contract Web design for my new company. They agreed, and off we went. I was the businessperson, the face of the company—the project manager, the sales force, the accountant. This let Leslie and Jason do what they were strong at: Web design and development.

We were definitely onto something. Our customers appreciated that we looked professional, spoke their language, and were focused on acting like a real business, not a fraternity organization. We also produced some of the best designed and valuable websites in our industry. Our first three clients were three of the most notable businesses and organizations in the city. I soon hired Leslie full time, and as the business grew I hired seven additional employees.

> *"I was under the impression that as long as I kept the pipeline full of sales, everything else would take care of itself."*

Sawt, Inc., saw great success. We grew from a business run out of a bedroom in my parents' house to a small company with offices in San Antonio and Houston. However, growth is challenging. More clients created a need for more people, which created a need for more software, desks, computers, health insurance, payroll taxes, office space, phone systems, and a multitude of other items and changes for which I was not prepared.

Cash flow was something I had never thought of—I was a salesperson. I was under the impression that as long as I kept the pipeline full of sales, everything else would take care of itself. I was unprepared for client delays on projects or customers not paying their bills. I was unsure of what to do when our office literally flooded and we were left without a functional work environment for more than a week.

I was twenty-two years old now, and my friends were getting prepared for college graduation, partying every weekend, and having the time of their lives. I was concerned with a slumping economy in the post-9/11 reality, clients who owed tens of thousands of dollars, and how I was going to make payroll. But I probably could have avoided most of these problems and headaches.

When I started the business at age nineteen in my parents' house, a lot of people assumed that my parents had funded the company or were helping me run it. My dad was a successful businessman, and my parents had always provided my sister and me with the greatest educational opportunities and a nice place to live. I will admit, I did not come from hard times or poverty. I must give credit to both my parents, who came from working-class backgrounds yet were able to provide me with a nice lifestyle.

My great mistake was being so stubborn and intent on proving to everyone that this was my company that I separated the company from my parents as much as I could. My parents were two extremely valuable resources at my disposal, and both of them were willing to help, but I failed to use them. This strategy worked fine for the first two years of business, as nothing seemed to go wrong. But as challenges mounted and added up, I stayed too proud to ask for help.

What I learned from that experience was invaluable. I may have proven a point, but I believe that with the guidance and help of my parents, I would still be running Sawt, Inc., today. I only wish that I had been a bit older, wiser, and more experienced before I found myself in charge of an organization that grew so quickly. It might still be around today if I would have known then what I know now. But isn't that always the case?

Richard E. Sorensen, PhD

Dean of Pamplin College of Business
VIRGINIA TECH

Many of today's young professionals have the educational background and experience they need in order to be successful in the world of business. But by nature, young professionals typically are recently hired and new to an organization. Because of their age and relative lack of experience, they feel that it is inappropriate for them to take the initiative or to request additional levels of responsibility.

My advice to young professionals is to learn to accept opportunities as they arise. Look for opportunities to present themselves, and always take advantage of them. Things may not be exactly what you are preparing for, and situations may arise more quickly than you had anticipated. But you should never say, "I am not ready yet," because you probably are ready. These opportunities may never occur again, especially if you develop a reputation for turning things down.

From my own experience, after graduating with a Bachelor of Science degree in electrical engineering from Brooklyn's Polytechnic University and being commissioned in the U.S. Army Corp of Engineers, I had the opportunity to serve as a commissioned lieutenant with an Army construction engineer battalion in both Okinawa and then Vietnam during 1965 and 1966. Previously, the battalion had been providing post-support activities at Fort Stewart, Georgia, which at that time served as a National Guard summer training camp. As is typical during peacetime, the battalion did not previously have the resources or opportunities to be engaged in extensive construction projects.

So when these construction opportunities presented themselves, many of the long-term experienced officers found themselves unprepared for the new challenges. I was less prepared than they were, but I did not let this deter me. Instead of worrying about what I did not know, I recognized some of the similarities between problems that we were facing and things that I was already familiar with, and I figured out the rest. I was later recognized for my actions by being awarded the Bronze Star for meritorious service and being offered a regular Army commission.

This experience carried over to my serving as a manager with a company that is now known as Verizon, and then to the completion of my MBA and PhD. Furthermore, I became a faculty member and business school dean at the age of thirty. This same attitude of jumping right in whether or not I felt I was "ready" has continued to serve me well over the years.

Great Mistake #2: Dictating, Not Empowering

As I mentioned in the first chapter, I founded the organization Young Execs in San Antonio. In one year's time, it grew from just an idea to an organization of more than one hundred members. Our very first luncheon event had fifty young professionals and featured a panel discussion of three local leaders. Our one-year anniversary luncheon was attended by more than one hundred twenty people, including city leaders and some of the area's most talented young professionals. Our keynote speaker was billionaire and philanthropist Red McCombs. The luncheon was a symbol of growth and success in a short amount of time. I adopted a goal of adding new Young Execs chapters throughout Texas. The second chapter was targeted for Austin.

Today, the chapter that I founded in Austin is alive and doing very well, yet the San Antonio chapter is no longer in existence. So how did the Young Execs in my hometown die, whereas the chapter in Austin continues to thrive?

In 2003, the idea for Young Execs came about through my frustration in not finding an organization dedicated to young professionals. I had been to many chambers of commerce, business associations, and civic groups, hoping to meet young people in business—without luck. While I have found great value in chambers and in organizations such as the American Marketing Association or the Public Relations Society of America, young professionals did not constitute even a small percentage of their members.

My goal was to create an organization that accomplished three things. The first was the building of relationships among the future leaders of San Antonio. Like many other cities, San Antonio has a "good ol' boys" network—a group of CEOs, executives, and leaders in a community who seem to make things happen and lead initiatives. Although the term is gender specific, the network has changed and is no longer made up only of males. My thought was "Why not start building those relationships as young professionals, instead of waiting until we are older?" (You may recognize this concept from the chapter "Find Mentors and Create Fans.")

The second goal of Young Execs was to create educational opportunities. This included everything from hosting speakers at luncheons to facilitating dinnertime conversations with moderators (all part of the Soak It Up concept).

The third and final goal of Young Execs was to encourage community involvement. At every function, we had representatives from nonprofit organizations speak about volunteer opportunities or have someone from the city speak about civic involvement (a concept you'll recognize in a later chapter, "Be Selfish and Volunteer").

I still believe that the accomplishment of these three goals as our mission for Young Execs was spot-on. However, it was the way in which I founded and grew the organization that determined its long-term success.

I love creating things from scratch. If it's a business, a concept, or anything at all, I receive the greatest satisfaction from seeing a simple idea turn into real success. When I have an idea that I believe has merit, it usually consumes me. Thank goodness, Lacey has now become accustomed to these times of extreme focus; she knows that it is probably best to leave me alone as I become immersed in an ideal and achieving a goal. It was a battle, but she finally allowed me to put up dry-erase whiteboards in our home office so that I could diagram my many ideas. When I thought up Young Execs, I had the idea and the concept all mapped out. The vision, the mission statement, the organizational structure, and every aspect of Young Execs—it was all ready to go. As the founder, I became president of the organization for the first year and would pass the reins over the following year.

After scheduling the first luncheon, I had a meeting with some of the young professionals who I thought could be of value to the organization in leadership roles. I envisioned specific people for certain roles and was able to spell out to them exactly what was expected of their role and their tasks. Although they were well qualified to handle their specific roles, none of them met my expectations. I was constantly filling in and taking up the slack. I was basically running the organization by myself.

It was a hugely successful first year. However, I did not recognize the problem, even though it was the elephant in the room: I was spending almost twenty hours a week on an organization that produced zero income for me. The organization was growing, young professionals were getting a great deal of value out of their involvement, and I gained exposure in the community for founding the organization.

After I stepped down as president, I began my focus on expansion, beginning with a chapter in Austin. Phil Rodriguez, an Austin resident who did business in San Antonio and attended Young Execs events there, was a great candidate to help lead the charge in Austin. Phil had a large network and showed the passion and entrepreneurial spirit required to take on the role as president of the Austin chapter. He gathered a team of young professionals for his leadership team.

Fast-forward one year. The San Antonio chapter had folded. The Austin chapter was alive, strong, and still growing. I had not been involved in either Young Execs chapter for many months. I decided to go back to school full time, which took all my time and left me unable to volunteer any time to either chapter. Although I was disappointed that Young Execs of San Antonio had come to an end, I remember thinking to myself, "Be happy for what you accomplished—it was an undertaking that could not have begun without you."

Fast-forward another six months. I was reading *Winning*, by Jack Welch—one of my favorite business books of all time. In his book, Welch speaks of leadership and what constitutes great and poor leadership. He says, "A great leader creates an organization that succeeds after the leader is no longer around." Well, this hit me like a ton of bricks. Had I failed with Young Execs of San Antonio? I'd created an effective organization that accomplished much in one year, and now Jack Welch is calling me a bad leader because it did not survive after I left? Wouldn't it make me a good leader that when I led the organization it did well?

As it turns out, Welch was correct. Although I was the founder and ran a series of events for one year, I failed at creating an organization that was bigger than me—that belonged to the young professionals and not to me. Young Execs of San Antonio did not succeed because I did not empower its leadership to succeed. I merely tried to use them to fulfill my dreams and my wishes, not their own. They had ideas of their own, but if it wasn't part of my plan, I did not let it have a place in the organization. I looked at them more as employees than as potential leaders.

In Austin, where I was not heavily involved, Phil Rodriguez led his team into a successful year and transition. He gave free reign to his young leaders so that they would try and succeed on their own. Because of this, the entire Young Execs of Austin organization—not just one person—has ownership and pride in what they accomplish. There is a collaborative approach; everyone is empowered to make changes and to lead. This is why this chapter is still around today.

Fast-forward one more time, five years later. The nonprofit organization San Antonio Sports had asked me to serve as one of the founding members of its Circle of Champions. This group was to be composed of young leaders in the San Antonio community to help raise awareness and funding for the nonprofit. The group started off with excitement, but as with any new organization or group, there was no clearly defined mission, and it soon lost momentum.

I believed the Circle of Champions had great potential benefit for San Antonio Sports, however, and I had ideas and a plan that I felt could define a mission and energize the young leaders. I asked if I could lead a meeting, and my request was granted. I had a plan, and I felt it would be a success if I implemented it "as is"—but I knew from my experience with Young Execs that I had to approach this differently. I wanted to empower my fellow members and ensure their buy-in. I could have outlined a plan as specific as I had with Young Execs, but I knew that doing so would be a grave mistake for the organization.

So I called Erik Darmstetter, CEO of Sales By 5, and asked if he would be willing to facilitate a brainstorming session for the members of the Circle of Champions. I wanted everyone to get a sense of empowerment and equal contribution. Erik agreed that my original plan could be great for the Circle of Champions, but accepted the goal of facilitating a beneficial brainstorming session, not determining what plan should or should not be used.

The brainstorming session began, and the desires, goals, and strengths of our members were clarified. The ideas that were coming from the members in this meeting matched my original plan exactly. I thought to myself, "This is great! We are going to do exactly what I originally wanted and planned, but everyone feels as if this is a collaborative plan instead of just mine. I've avoided the mistake I made with Young Execs!"

But this brainstorming session went on to become a success beyond what I hoped for. Someone soon offered a great idea that I never thought of. Then another person took that idea, expanded it, and made it better. Another member jumped in enthusiastically and improved on that idea. Soon the collaborative process took the group in a whole different direction, to a place that was not within my plan, and it was amazing! We'd stumbled onto something that made us excited about our group. We were all energized about the direction of the Circle of Champions because of a collaborative effort that was more than the plan I had in mind. My original plan may have been good and could have worked well, but our new direction was much better.

> "*Empowerment is truly the most beneficial thing we can do as leaders.*"

The value in empowering people is not just that they feel empowered—it is that empowerment is truly the most beneficial thing we can do as leaders. The value of collaboration is that the ideas produced by many people working together will be much better ideas than those of just one person. If you find yourself in a leadership position where you are making large decisions for an organization, you can apply this principle—but you can also apply it to any project or task that involves more people than just you.

Jason Brand

Former President, Pacific Rim
MERRILL LYNCH & CO.

Young professionals need to guard against becoming and remaining generalists. In many industries, being "a jack of all trades and a master of none" can be very dangerous—avoid this trap.

Build credibility as quickly as possible.

Instead, your primary objective when starting out should be to build credibility as quickly as possible. This will lead to broader recognition of your skills and, with further assignments, the development of actual expertise in a specific field.

For instance, at an early stage, a new professional shouldn't be shy about accepting responsibility for a task. This is not about attempting to lead a project overall—that will be done by a senior colleague—but rather about getting to lead part of a project. When a boss has asked you to produce a document or other deliverable, while fulfilling this task you may hit upon a better way to present the information. Suggesting the improvement to your senior adds to your credibility, makes him or her look good, and will likely lead to further assignments—all of which eventually leads to recognition for your over time.

Developing a rewarding career is a progression. First, build credibility so you are given chances to develop and deepen expertise in an area. Look next for a second, related area to develop an additional capability. Credit for your work will come naturally and your firm will continue to expose you to challenges that further your development.

Young professionals often feel the need to show their knowledge, prove themselves, or ensure that they get credit and recognition for their work. Although it is important for you to have documented success in your workplace, try to find that balance: getting the recognition you deserve without being a dictator. Doing what is in the best interest of your organization typically ends up being in your own individual interest as well.

John Meyer
President & CEO
ACXIOM CORPORATION

When you're starting off, it's best to focus on the experiences more than the financials.

Experience is your second education (the difference is that you get paid for it rather than paying for it). Like your mom told you, no one can ever take your education from you. Same with experience. How many times have you heard about a person who is a great accountant or technical person but who has reached a plateau in his or her progression? It is because that person has had too few experiences and therefore has limited opportunities.

> Experience is your second education.

It is better to be good at many things rather than an expert in just one. A one-legged stool has trouble standing for very long. Add more legs to your stool.

When everyone says, "That job is a mess, and I would not do it," run to it! If it is a mess, there is only one way to take it—up. Conversely, when it is a well-performing role, down or status quo is the only way to go.

A career in business is like sports for adults. Be competitive, and play at business with the same enthusiasm.

Great Mistake #3: Getting Too Big for Your Britches
When people ask me what the number one problem of young professionals is, I respond with the same answer I would give if asked about the number one problem of middle-aged professionals or any other professional—ego. My dad always refers to this as being "too big for your britches."

I dedicated an earlier chapter to ego ("Don't Believe the Hype"). But as you can see, this is a problem that keeps popping up, in almost every chapter. Great Mistake #1 was that I was too proud to ask for help—that was ego. Great Mistake #2 was that I wanted to take credit and be recognized as the sole leader of an organization—that was ego. An ego can ruin businesses, it can ruin teams, and it can ruin careers.

Is it more important for people to think you are a successful young professional or for you to be a successful young professional? This may come down to your definition of success. I was recognized more for my success during my Sawt, Inc., days than I am today, and yet there is no comparison between then and now. I had limited success back then in the big scheme of things; what I actually had was a successful image. I have no fanfare now as I did back then, but now I am a partner in an incredible marriage, I appreciate a great family and friends, I live in a terrific home, I'm in better physical shape, and I'm blessed to be part of the wonderful community of St. Helena's Church in Boerne, Texas. Did you notice the Five Fs of success in there? My greatest mistake could have been the lack of an accurate definition of success in the early part of my career—but this also was created by my ego. I was more concerned with appearing successful than with actually being a success.

Lacey and I were friends for a couple of years before we began to date. She knew me during my Sawt, Inc., days, and today she jokes that I used to be "King Kohnen." We were friends, but without hesitation she will say that she sensed an arrogance in me that bothered her. Her assessment was true. My priorities were very different. My Fs of success leaned more toward Ferraris, fame, and fortune—I never really achieved any of those, but that was what I thought I wanted.

> *"In every decision you make, ask yourself, 'Am I doing this for myself or for others?'"*

As competitive individuals, we will never get rid of our ego altogether. Lacey still questions some of my decisions and asks if I'm doing things for the right reasons. This is and will continue to be an everlasting challenge. A simple test may help you to see whether something is just about ego: in every decision you make, ask yourself, "Am I doing this for myself or for others?"

For example, when I was running Sawt, Inc., my dream car was a Mercedes CLK430. Even though I liked it because it would be luxurious and fun, it was more appealing to me because of the image. I wanted people to see me in that car. I probably would've parked it in the front of every parking lot and slowly gotten in and out so everyone could see me! That is ego influencing a decision. I was very close to buying this car, which would've used up a significant amount of my income. But I was willing to stretch my financial situation in order to achieve this image. So think about it: when you decide to buy that BMW or that Rolex, are you really doing it for yourself or for others to see? If even the slightest bit of your decision is based on the opinion of others, your ego is beginning to cloud your decision-making process.

Bob Morgan
President
CHARLOTTE CHAMBER OF COMMERCE

We hear all the time that young professionals today—the "creative class"—graduate from college and look for a place to live first, and then seek a job.

In 1996, however, a couple of graduates from St. Bonaventure University in upstate New York called on the Charlotte Chamber of Commerce. Their self-described mission: "Atlanta is hosting the Olympics this year, and we are looking for the next up-and-coming Sun Belt city to make our home." It was a rather mature and insightful way to conduct a search for a job and a home.

Ultimately, they chose Charlotte, took entry-level jobs, and shared an apartment. Shortly after, each of them landed a job as an IT recruiter for a large employer. What they did was to create a pipeline. Within three years, more than thirty fellow alums, family members, and friends had followed these two to Charlotte. Twelve years later, the number has grown to more than two hundred. Certainly Charlotte has benefited from their presence. They have found economic opportunity and an attractive quality of life in a place that they now call home. Several, all from New York, have met in Charlotte and gotten married and are now starting families together.

To me, this is significant in that the two original pioneers were really outside the box in terms of how they made a post-graduation decision—a decision that has had a major influence on their own lives and now on the lives of literally hundreds of others.

These young professionals, just out of college, took a big risk—and it paid off. They thought outside the box and were willing to put in the time required to build a successful foundation, which than expanded. Former mayor Lee Clancey recalls what it's like to take that type of risk on a much higher level, and shares some important advice about considering the consequences.

Lee Clancey

Retired CEO, CEDAR RAPIDS AREA CHAMBER OF COMMERCE
Former Mayor of Cedar Rapids, Iowa

I believe that one of the most fundamental attributes a person needs to be successful is a willingness to take calculated risks, and to accept losses when they come—for inevitably, they will. To do things that others would never contemplate not only sets people apart, but gives them an edge. Taking risks is one of the true ways in which people can extend their comfort zones and learn new things about themselves. To do things that others dare not do is a growth experience that allows people to have a broader understanding of others and the world around them.

> What's the worst that could happen?

I have a pretty simple test that I give myself when confronted with a risk. I ask myself one question: "What is the worst thing that could happen?" Most times people don't take a risk because they are afraid, and yet many times, if asked, they cannot tell you what it is that they fear. Asking yourself about the worst thing that might happen will help you to articulate your fears, and usually you will discover that they are unfounded.

In 1996, I was serving as our downtown association's executive director. I interacted with our city council on a regular basis because of the downtown projects that were being jointly funded by the city and downtown property owners. That summer, our mayor decided not to run for reelection; the two leading candidates were existing council members who were part of a very contentious, argumentative council team. Personally, I believed our community deserved better.

However, no one more qualified stepped forward to run against these two candidates. I thought long and hard about whether or not to run for that position myself. While I had broad networks and plenty of name recognition due to our peculiar form of full-time city government, no woman had ever even served on the city council, much less as mayor. It was a very daunting proposition for me, especially given the fact that I had never run for public office. The tenor of political campaigns in America is not particularly inviting for candidates.

So I asked myself what might be the worst thing that could happen. The answer was not so bad: I might lose a very public race and some money, and I might have some nasty things said about me. But I would still have my family, my friends, and a job that I really loved. With my safety net in place, I threw my hat into the proverbial ring—and surprised myself and many others by winning.

As I quickly learned, becoming mayor was only the beginning. Running a city of 125,000 is no easy task. Every day brought a new challenge. For six years, I ran our city, and despite the stress, long hours, and risk, it is still to this day the greatest professional experience I have ever had. It was terrifying and adrenaline producing, but in the long run it was a wonderful experience to hold a title that allowed me to leverage my ability to do great things for my community.

So get out there. Take a risk. What's the worst thing that could happen?

You might be surprised!

In any industry there are norms. It is normal for car dealerships to advertise heavily on television. It is normal for mobile telephone companies to treat their potential customers better than their current ones (have you noticed that, too?). It is normal for sales professionals to visit a prospect's office when they want to sell something.

So what do you do that is normal within your industry? Why do you do it? Is it because this is the best possible solution or option for you and your organization? Or do you do it simply because that is what is "normal," because everybody does it that way? Why rock the boat, right?

What if a car dealership stopped spending money on television commercials and hired door-to-door sales professionals? Crazy, right? Or is it? What if mobile phone companies actually started giving their existing customers deals on new phones? You have to agree with that one at least—surely there is no better way to ensure satisfied customers. What if sales professionals asked their prospects to come to their office instead? That is, "If you want me to show you something valuable to your business, you need to come see me." It could be just a crazy concept—or it could be something that produces unique or different results. These results could be bad,

> *"Do I do this because it is just the way things are done? Or do I do this because it is the best option or solution?"*

but then again, nobody achieves greatness without experiencing a few failures.

One of the greatest ways to become known in your organization is to improve not only your job but also the jobs of others in your organization. Look to your company and your current job. What do you do just because it is the norm? What could you do differently? Try to think of everything, from how you answer the phone to how you dress to your filing system to where and when you eat lunch—include anything that is a part of your daily workday. It is actually pretty revealing when you start looking at everything and asking, "Do I do this because it is just the way things are done? Or do I do this because it is the best option or solution?"

As a young professional or someone new to an organization, you have an amazing opportunity to establish yourself as a leader and innovator in your company. If you do not understand why something is done a certain way, or if you think you know of a better way, ask your manager, "What are the reasons this is done this way?"

> "*The word 'why' puts people on the defensive—they feel they have to justify themselves.*"

Approaching this properly is of utmost importance. Never ask, "Why is this being done?" First of all, the manager may be the reason it is being done this way. Second, the very word "why" automatically puts people on the defensive—they feel they have to justify themselves or their actions. Finally, remember that assumptions are the major fault of all communication. There may be a perfectly good reason that something is done a certain way, even though you may not have thought of it.

By asking the question "What are the reasons this is done this way?" you will elicit one of two different responses. The first is "We do it this way because of XYZ valid reason," in which case you should move on and keep an eye out for your next opportunity to change things for the better. However, the second possible answer could be "I'm not really sure why we do it this way." If that is the case, then seize the opportunity—Jump In! You may stumble onto something that changes not only your job but also the jobs of everyone on your team and quite possibly everyone in the company.

John Younger
President & CEO
ACCOLO, INC.

I have started four companies, which is to say that I have made more mistakes than most people. Here are a few gems I have learned along the way.

1. **Focus on producing something that is valued by others, and do so with as few resources as you can.** I have been misdirected into thinking that I needed to raise a great deal of money before the technology or solution could be developed or released. Instead, test the underlying concepts first. Do this manually if possible. Companies that raise too much money before they have a viable business model end up spending too much money on marketing and are generally out of business as soon as the money runs out.

2. **Take time to play in the "CEO sandbox."** This is a piece of virtual real estate where the CEO can try new strategies, ideas, and structures in a contained and risk-free way. In the CEO sandbox, I give myself and all others involved with these projects full freedom to fail. Of course, that is not the desired intent,

but the structure is empowering and wonderful ideas are killed early, if necessary. Items in the sandbox must graduate before they can be incorporated into the company core.

3. **Manage people by the numbers, and be fair and decisive when making decisions about where people fit**. When working with people you really like, it can be difficult to know if and when they are no longer able to grow with the company. Keeping someone in a role where he or she is clearly struggling sends a clear message to your top performers that mediocrity is acceptable. This can be particularly difficult when your friends were the core of the company in an earlier stage. Remember that these decisions are not personal, and use data to drive your discussions.

4. **Balance the engines**. I have come up with a system that is grounded in the understanding that every company is like a rocket with four engines. The absolute value of any engine is not as important as the balancing of the four. They are:

   - Sales & Marketing (getting business)
   - Client Services (delivering on what was sold)
   - Technology Development and Support (feeding resources into the company's strategic differentiator)
   - Finance & Accounting (making sure that cash is managed properly and payroll can be made)

   This system has become invaluable to me in terms of managing a business.

In addition to reading business books, I also read the occasional biography or success story to learn the secrets to the success of CEOs and other leaders. One of those books was titled *Jump*

In, by Mark Burnett. The executive producer and creator of television blockbusters *Survivor*, *The Amazing Race*, and *The Ultimate Challenge*, Burnett is often recognized as the person responsible for the reality television craze.

The title of Burnett's book is a term he says he lives by, and it's how he raises his children. He says, "If you are going to learn how to swim, you have to jump in! If you are going to go for something big, sometimes you just have to close your eyes and jump in!" This really sums up and expresses the point of the current chapter. You may not feel ready. You are going to make mistakes. You may be taking a risky step or a moving away from the norm. But seizing whatever opportunities that come your way—and using the resources at hand to make the most of them—is the best way for a young professional to learn from the present and move toward a better future. Jump In! The only way to go is forward.

BLOG ME:
ypsuccess.com
Share your
thoughts.

LEAD FROM THE BOTTOM
Lead now! Think positively and create solutions.

Jim Goodnight

Chief Executive Officer

SAS

Find an employer who values everyone's contributions and recognizes that great ideas can come from anywhere in the organization.

SAS's business is producing knowledge in the form of software that solves problems. SAS doesn't require a huge amount of capital investment. Our most valuable assets are our people, because only creative people can troubleshoot and solve problems, write complex software algorithms, and create value.

One of our industry-focused products, SAS Anti-Money Laundering, was the idea of a sales account executive who recognized opportunity in the financial services market. Creative people work for the love of a challenge. They like the feeling of accomplishment that comes from solving a problem, whether it's technical, artistic, or social.

We've discovered that creative capital is generated every time there's an interaction between an employee and a customer. Consultants and technical support staff don't just troubleshoot— they collaborate with customers to invent new solutions. Salespeople don't just sell software—they build long-term relationships and, in the process, learn surprising things about their customers' needs.

But anyone at SAS can make a difference.

Recently, one of our landscapers asked me how his department could make a difference. I told him that he was already making a difference; in fact, through his department's efforts to make our head-

> ---
> Great ideas can come from anywhere.

quarters look its best, they were helping with every sale we make. When customers, government officials, and other visitors come to our company headquarters, the first thing they see is our campus, which is representative of our creativity, our attention to detail, and our stability.

I have never been afraid to lead. At nineteen, I started a Web development business and led a team of eight employees toward production, efficiency, and (sometimes) profitability. At twenty-three, I started Young Execs, an organization of young professionals focused on building long-term relationships and involvement in the community. For seven years, I had an after-work gig leading youth sports teams as a high school and middle school baseball and basketball coach.

I am often asked, "What happened in your development that gave you the confidence to lead, especially at a young age?" But it wasn't until a few years ago, when I was volunteering as a teacher for the nonprofit organization Junior Achievement, that I finally was able to pinpoint the time in my life when I began to develop leadership behaviors and confidence.

After joining Junior Achievement, I was assigned to a sixth-grade class at a low-income public school. I asked each of the students, "What do you want to do when you grow up?"

Their answers shocked me.

One boy shrugged and said, "I don't know, whatever job I can get."

Three other students also replied, "I don't know."

A few others responded that they wanted the same occupation as their father or mother had.

I was expecting the wide-eyed imagination that one might expect from sixth-graders: professional baseball player, doctor, astronaut, scientist. But these students were limited by their environment. Their dreams were limited to what they had experienced in their lives.

This made me think about my own dreams at that age, and I realized that indeed there had been a defining moment when it all changed for me. It was at TMI–The Episcopal School of Texas, a private college preparatory school in San Antonio, which I began attending my junior year in high school. Immediately upon starting at TMI, I noticed an environment of success and leadership.

Founded in 1893, the school has a history of educating future leaders, from senators and political figures to CEOs and industry leaders. Even the faculty had a background of success. My senior English teacher and present-day friend, Bob Bell, was a professor at the United States Military Academy at West Point. (I am sure his copy of the book will be filled with red marks.)

> "*The environment you find yourself in can either limit your mind-set or help you realize great things are possible.*"

My defining moment was when I took my first leadership role at TMI. I was nominated to be president of the Fellowship of Christian Athletes. That was all it took. I gained confidence and was able to experience a role as a leader at a very young age. From that point forward, I was drawn to leadership positions.

I didn't realize what a pivotal experience it had been, however, until that day in the Junior Achievement class. The answers given by those kids made me realize that the environment you find yourself in (or put yourself in) can either limit your mind-set or help you realize that great things are possible. Being in an environment of success, one that encouraged leadership, helped change my mind-set from that of a follower to that of a leader. These students whom I had taught for eight weeks were limited in their vision of success because their surroundings did not encourage dreams of success. If you ask students at schools like TMI what they want to do when they grow up, you'll find that their vision is optimistic and limitless.

David C. Achim
President & CEO
ROME CORPORATION

The best advice I can give young professionals is: "Never confuse effort with results."

In other words, effort is required to achieve results, but effort without results does not secure success. Thinking that you are doing your job or making progress by just making an effort, and blaming the lack of success on other factors, deceives you into a place that prevents real success from breaking through into your life.

Never confuse effort with results.

Some of you may be thinking, "Well, not all of us were able to attend a top-tier private school and benefit from an environment of success." It's true, I was extremely fortunate to have been in that environment at an early age, and I am grateful to my parents for sacrificing certain luxuries and going to great lengths to afford my sister and I these educational opportunities. However, the importance of this concept is that anyone can create a similar environment in their own life, once they are able to grasp the very real difference that a positive, stimulating setting can make.

When you graduate from college and start a career, nobody drops you off in an environment of success. You have to create your own environment. This is where building your network of friends and colleagues comes into play, along with finding your mentors.

By keeping highly motivated people in your life and limiting your contact with people who just go through the motions of life, you will end up creating your own successful environment.

Mike Thompson

President & CEO
GROUPWARE TECHNOLOGY, INC.

The sooner you realize that your employees—your people—are your most valuable asset and are a major differentiator in your business, the quicker you will achieve success.

It is critically important to surround yourself with good people—people who are talented, capable, and experienced. Embrace diversity and seek out people who have different professional and personal experiences. Often this diversity provides your business with a unique perspective and competitive advantage that you will be able to utilize repeatedly.

Most important, find people whom you can trust—although it's paramount to remember that trust doesn't always mean agreement. Trust means that your people will tell the truth in a situation, even if they know that you will not like it. This kind of trust is difficult to find but invaluable when you do. Trust requires open communication; do not shy away from the difficult conversations. People may not like to hear what you have to say, but they will respect you for saying it.

> Seek out people with different experiences.

Empower your people to do their jobs, and then get out of their way! Of course, you can mentor and lead them, but it's equally important that you give them the responsibility to solve problems in your business. This attitude and the subsequent behavior provide your people with opportunities to grow, both professionally and personally.

Finally, make sure that your people share in the successes of the company.

There is no shortage of opinions, theories, self-help guides, and advice on leadership—all of which will help you cultivate good people and create an environment for success. In fact, if you type the term "leadership" in the Books section of Amazon.com, you will come up with several hundred thousand hits. However, among all those, one particular title stands out as a statement of opportunity for every young professional. It's by Lee Iacocca, the retired chairman and CEO of the Chrysler Corporation, and it's called *Where Have All the Leaders Gone?*

Much like Iacocca, I feel there is a shortage of great leadership. One can observe this shortage everywhere in business, from the corporate world to the nonprofit world. In regards to leadership for CEOs or executive management of major corporations, there are far greater experts out there than myself. But one thing I do know: leadership doesn't have to come from the top. In fact, the focus of this chapter is on young professionals who are not yet in a designated leadership role.

How can you establish yourself as a leader and practice leadership if you are twenty-five years old and no one reports to you?

Matthew Schissler shares a personal story about defining your own career path, creating opportunities for yourself, and getting into the right position; however, he also makes a bold statement on "paycheck players" that should motivate you regarding potential leadership opportunities. Schissler suggests that CEOs have to admit and understand that although they may want a company full of superstars, the reality is that every company will be filled with a large number of paycheck players and only a few superstars.

So how do we differentiate ourselves as a leader as opposed to a paycheck player?

Matthew L. Schissler
Chairman & CEO
CORD BLOOD AMERICA

My advice has its roots in a quote by Bill Brooks, famed motivational speaker and former football coach. One of Bill's famous quotes is "You have to be in position to be in position." Far too often, especially with today's younger workforce, you see the presiding motivation coming from outside influences and not from the work itself. Many of our young staffers provide adequate work, but put in little extra effort to really succeed.

We call them "paycheck players." They are here just to earn a check; they come in by 8:00 a.m., leave by 5:00 p.m., and perform just enough work that they won't be let go. As a CEO, we accept this, pay them adequately, and expect mediocre performance. We book this performance for what it is worth, and move on to hire additional people, hoping to find the superstars every company desires.

It is easy for a company to say, "We look to hire all superstars," or, "You have to have a little something extra to work here." However, if every company stood behind this mantra, none of us would have any employees to do the work.

A young professional needs to understand that employers are hungry for new employees who can give them "more than average," even though their mantra may be that they already employ only above-average talent. This is especially true of midsized growth companies with little brand recognition. Truth be told, most employers

> You have to be in position to be in position.

believe in the beginning that all their hires are above average, only to be disappointed more often than not.

So how do young job seekers get "in position"? Rather than focus on a few core companies they believe they would like to work for, they need to expand their options to a multitude of midsized companies that have good growth track records but may not be household names. These are the companies where young professionals have more of an opportunity to advance quickly, earn higher-than-average income, and be in a position to take advantage of the company's growth coupled with their own ambition.

How do I know? I was one of them.

I took a job at age twenty-three with a technical staffing company. I never had a lick of technical training. But I saw that the company was growing quickly, could tell they were straining for good talent, and recognized quickly that the compensation could skyrocket if I put in a better-than-average effort.

While all my friends went to work for the "big six" accounting firms or went into pharmaceutical sales—which do show good, healthy returns over very long periods of time—I chose a different, not-so-beaten path. I did my due diligence and found that the company was healthy financially, growing quickly, and excelling in a hot market at the time. But the company did not have high earners to point to, as it was still too new to have them in place.

To make a long story short, at age twenty-five, I was running the largest business unit; by age twenty-eight, I was managing a P&L of more than $30 million dollars. I earned more than $180,000 per year with this young upstart, which eventually was bought by a Fortune 500 company. At acquisition time, I cashed out on my many stock options and used the money to start my own business...seven years ago.

The moral is simple: none of this would have been possible if I went the easy route that many of my friends did. Today, each of them has a nice living and a family, as I do, but they will never have the life-changing moment that I had and will forever cherish.

To be "in position," young professionals must research many more opportunities than what traditionally stares them in the face. They must go on many interviews and, even after accepting a job, keep good relations across multiple industries and companies. With those connections, they will be "in position" when a midsized growth opportunity strikes.

Being "in position"—willing and available to make different decisions and to do what it takes to stand out from your peers—is certainly a head start. The biggest challenge in leadership for young professionals, however, is finding a way to be a leader when there is already a designated leader in place. For most of us starting out in our careers, this is the situation. You have a manager, and your manager may have a manager, and so on. So how do you become a leader when that is not your specified role? How do you avoid being a paycheck player? It is easier than you think.

> "*Wherever you find problem people and everyday problems, you'll also find a chance to take the lead.*"

First of all, among organizations of at least twenty people, it would be hard to find one that does not have at least one employee who is a naysayer, complainer, or negative force; these are "problem people." In addition, no matter the size of the organization, every team experiences everyday problems. These are your two opportunities, the two slam-dunk issues to attack as a young professional: problem people and everyday problems. Wherever you find one or both of these factors, you'll also find a chance to take the lead.

Lee Clancey

Retired CEO, CEDAR RAPIDS AREA CHAMBER OF COMMERCE

Former Mayor of Cedar Rapids, Iowa

Career Killers I have seen include things like grammatical errors in cover letters and resumes. Others are gum chewing, less-than-professional dress, and annoying mannerisms in interviews. Once a person is hired, a new set of Career Killers awaits: rarely, if ever, volunteering for "other duties as assigned"; personal and often inappropriate use of technology while working; a less-than-stellar work ethic; tardiness to work; delayed responses to e-mail, letters, phone messages, etc. The people who create these minor problems are never going to succeed when the big problems come along.

Let's start with the everyday problems that occur in every organization. The first instinct when a problem occurs is to complain about it, blame someone, or panic. This is a normal reaction for paycheck players, but leaders can emerge based on how they deal with problems. When everything is going well, it is easy for everyone to feel good, make great decisions, and be model employees. It is in the face of adversity that leaders step forward and shine.

It's hard to imagine that everyone would not want to be a problem solver, but remember the mind-set of a paycheck player—they do only what is necessary to keep their jobs, collect their paychecks, and go home. They will not be looking to create more work for themselves.

This is your golden opportunity. This is where you take the lessons of the previous chapter, "Jump In!"—and go for it. Be someone in your organization who is constantly seeking better ways to do things or trying to solve problems. Go to your manager with ideas and solutions. Ask your teammates for feedback on some of your ideas. While others are just sitting back and complaining, become known as someone who instead actively looks for solutions.

A few years ago I was working with a sales team and a marketing team, integrating them into one team. The majority of these new teammates were extremely negative when it came to combining the teams. One employee felt that sales and marketing were separate functions; another was concerned about who was going to be the manager, since previously there was both a director of sales and a director of marketing. They were behaving like problem people.

I had a half-day meeting with the team and the CEO of the company to explain the team's new role and to outline expectations and how things would work. Negativity spread throughout the early-morning sessions, and frustration set in. We were anticipating a positive meeting, expecting that these individuals would become a team ready to conquer the world. But all we were getting was pushback from the employees: "That won't work" and "This is not smart" and "I don't feel comfortable with that."

Finally, the newest and youngest member of the team spoke up. Julie was twenty-three or twenty-four years old and had been with the organization less than six months. Throughout the meeting, she had been very quiet, but at this point she single-handedly changed the entire morning—and potentially, the entire makeup of the team.

Julie began pointing out the positive aspects of combining the sales and marketing teams. She began presenting solutions to some of the problems that her teammates had brought up. Negative thoughts are contagious, but positive thinking can also be contagious. The switch of thinking from negative to positive, and the voicing of potential solutions instead of problems, made all the difference in laying the groundwork for the team.

> "*A leader is someone who inspires people to move forward.*"

Julie simply did what was in the best interest of her team, but as you can imagine, this was not the only result: the CEO of the company had noticed her leadership. While others were unconstructive and wasted time complaining, Julie stepped up and became the leader of the team for that day with her positive attitude and problem-solving mind-set. And remember that she was the youngest and newest member of the team.

By defeating negative problem people with a positive attitude and defeating everyday problems with creative solutions, you can accomplish what Julie did and lead from the bottom. This is not as complicated and in-depth as any of those theories offered in the 300,000 titles on leadership from Amazon.com, but I can promise you that if you keep the following two concepts in mind, you will differentiate yourself from the paycheck players:

Concept #1: Think positive when others are negative.
Concept #2: Create solutions when others are complaining.

My simple definition of a leader is someone who inspires people to move forward. When observing your own behavior in meetings and at work, ask yourself, "Is my behavior helping us move forward? Am I inspiring or motivating others to do so?"

Cindi Bigelow
President
BIGELOW TEA COMPANY

I do not think there is any magic bullet when it comes to trying to develop yourself into the best leader possible. However, I do believe there are key points for young professionals who are trying not just to survive but to thrive in today's competitive environment.

Rule #1: Remember that people are watching you.

Whether you like it or not, you are a role model for those you work for and those around you. If you want only the very best from your team (and to succeed in today's challenging world, you can expect nothing else), you have to remember to be on your best behavior each and every day. You do not have the luxury of being moody, letting ego get in the way of good decisions, or having tantrums every once in a while. You set the standard that the rest of your team will follow. Although it is not an easy burden, you have to stay focused on that fact daily.

Rule #2: Solicit contrary opinion to that of your own.

This particular leadership skill is one of the most challenging and one of the most critical. Your team needs to know that you want and need to be challenged. You must look at things from different angles. Honor the naysayer and praise critical thinking. The more you challenge the programs and plans being considered, the better the chance of their success. Teach your team to honor critical thinking, and teach them how to nurture differences. Use all the ideas in the room to ensure that you have the best possible plan. You do not need people who think just like you do. One of you is enough!

Rule #3: Be active and give back to the community.

Giving back is a critical aspect of your development process. Face it: In the office, your team members have to listen to what you say, but outside your work environment, they don't. If you can become an effective leader in the community at large, you'll become a much stronger manager and leader inside your organization.

Support of community efforts sets the stage, portraying you as a good "role model" for those around you—and it is also very challenging! Getting a group of independent thinkers in a community situation to work together as a team is not easy, but the more you become respected and effective in the outside world, the better leader you become inside your organization!

Rule #4: Create a positive environment for your team.

If you don't create a positive environment, your team could easily be seduced away for monetary reasons. More important, setting a positive environment is the right thing to do morally. A good experience at the office usually means your colleagues go home and share that positive experience with their families. This in turn makes for the most productive managers and team members, because when employees come to work feeling good, they bring all of themselves to the office. When they feel good about walking in the office, they feel good about spreading their wings and trying to fly. This is the type of person who is going to help you move the organization forward. Positive employees join you in becoming the drivers of the business.

Cindi recommends *Soar with Your Strengths,* by Clifton and Nelson

So how do you get your team to give 100 percent? You set the tone as a good role model; you solicit different opinions from your own; you develop yourself as a leader in the outside community; and you create an environment where people feel positive.

It's tough out there, but with the right people by your side...
watch out, world! You are going to make things happen.

Are there other important rules to creating an environment
rich in success? Are there other ways to ensure that you are moving
the entire organization forward? I am sure the answer is yes! But I
also know this: without the elements described here, your path will
be much longer...Good luck, and more important, enjoy the journey.

My only sibling, my older sister Jennifer Kirsch, has seen
great success in her young career. Since achieving a management
role and working with younger employees, she has become a great
source of discussion and education regarding the same topics
addressed in this book. What surprised me the most about her
experience in management is how she has noticed the differences
between women and men in the workplace.

Jennifer Kohnen Kirsch
Marketing Professional

The following story took place during my first year out of college.
I was working at a large corporation (Motorola) as a procurement buyer, though I was in the process of moving into a position as a system and process efficiency manager.

Jennifer
invites you to
theMBAblog.com

    I graduated with a communications degree from a small liberal
arts school, and was hired into the Supply Management organization
at Motorola with five other young professionals who all majored in
supply chain management. I knew I was hired at a slightly lower salary than the rest of my colleagues due to my degree, but I figured that
for the first year I would learn and contribute as much as I could.

When the year was complete, I heard that my other colleagues had reviews with their managers, and most had received raises. My boss was on maternity leave, and the acting boss did not come to me about this. So I went to our Human Resources contact and inquired about my assessment and a potential raise. I recapped the results that I had produced and the leadership skills that I had demonstrated to encourage others to achieve.

Jennifer recommends **Elements of Style,** *by William Strunk, Jr.*

When asked how much I thought I deserved, I stated an amount that I thought was generous, based on market research. The HR person came back to me the next day and exceeded the amount.

The bottom line: go into your new job ready to prove what you can do. Be able to articulate the results you have achieved, and then assess and ask for your value.

One special note: because I have managed both males and females, I am aware that females typically do not talk about salary. So if you are a woman, while it may seem difficult, be sure to continuously assess your value and talk with your manager about it. You need to ensure that you are being paid a just and fair wage for the value that you bring in comparison to your male counterparts.

I learned from Jennifer that leading from the bottom can be particularly daunting for some women, who even today are encouraged to let others take the reins. But she is certainly not the only one to offer advice about this issue.

Hala Moddelmog

President & CEO

SUSAN G. KOMEN FOR THE CURE

Drive, determination, and superior performance are all qualities needed to succeed in business. These are not gender-based qualities; these are leadership qualities.

My advice to young women just entering the professional workforce is to set a goal, find a mentor who can guide you, then work smarter and harder than all your colleagues. The best way to move on to the next level is to do the job you are in to the very highest level, with full engagement in the organization. People will notice, and you will be rewarded.

And remember, if you are fortunate enough to do something first or lead the way, you must reach back and bring along those who helped you get there—otherwise you don't deserve to be where you are.

Once you've established yourself as a young leader and worked your way to the top, remember to reward those who also have found a way to lead from the bottom. This practice encourages good business and a healthy community, and can be very rewarding for you—both personally and professionally.

IT'S NOT WHAT YOU KNOW...
Build, maintain, and nurture your relationships in life and work.

11

On the first anniversary of the founding of Young Execs of San Antonio, we had a special luncheon featuring one of San Antonio's most prominent citizens. Billionaire and philanthropist Red McCombs was our keynote speaker, and his booming voice had everyone in the audience captivated as he told his story about going from auto mechanic's son to billionaire. In 2008, McCombs was estimated by *Forbes* magazine to be worth $1.6 billion.

McCombs began selling cars in 1950 and owned his first dealership by the age of twenty-five. Along with growing an automobile fortune, McCombs cofounded Clear Channel Communications, and he is nationally known as a former owner of the San Antonio Spurs and the Minnesota Vikings. In San Antonio and in the sports and business worlds, McCombs is a household name.

At our anniversary event, McCombs had great stories and plenty of wisdom to share, but my favorite line that day was a challenge to an age-old adage. Most of us have heard the line "It's not what you know, it's who you know." But McCombs corrected the saying: "It's not who you know. It's who knows you!" He got hearty applause and chuckles out of the crowd.

I love this quote, because while we may know the same number of people as Bill Gates or Warren Buffett, more people know Bill Gates and Warren Buffett. It's not who Bill Gates knows that matters; it's the fact that everyone knows Bill Gates. We should take baby steps here, even if everyone thinks they would like to end up one day as a recognizable business leader. After all, we have to start somewhere, and building personal relationships where both parties know each other is a great place to start.

Think back to the dinnertime conversation Lacey and I had with our friends the Klugers; we were discussing success at a young age. The most repeated comment made was that the key to success was building and maintaining relationships.

There are many articles and books on networking and building relationships, but my simple strategy for building a network is based on four elements:

1. Creating Your Network
2. Building and Growing Your Relationships
3. Maintaining Your Relationships
4. Calling on Your Network

Okay, so it's just a little more complicated than that; in steps number one and two, you need to consider two items: quantity and quality.

You know the old saying, "It's quality, not quantity"? That is partially correct, because in building your network, you want both. The larger your network, the larger your access to building more relationships and resources (Creating Your Network). The better your relationships are with that network (Building and Growing Your Relationships), the more value and access to resources you will have.

In each aspect of the four network-building steps, everything is based on providing mutual value. People you meet will need to find value in you, and you are looking to find value in them. The value could be as simple as talking to someone because he or she has a positive attitude, a wealth of knowledge, or some experience in a specific industry. On the flip side, people will want to build relationships with you based on which of these sorts of things you bring to them.

Ralph J. Schulz, Jr.
President & CEO
NASHVILLE AREA CHAMBER OF COMMERCE

Three bits of advice for young professionals:

1. Purposeful networking is all about advancing your cause while building relationships with people important to advancing the cause.
2. A wise man once told me, "It's not who you know or what you know, but who knows what you know that counts."
3. *Integrity* is indispensable to effectiveness. Integrity creates trust, and trust is relevant to all relationships.

CREATING YOUR NETWORK

Before you can establish quality networking relationships, obviously, you need to find people to include in your network. There are no limits to who can be in your network or how you build it. You create your own opportunities according to what works for you.

> Download my companion guide: *YP Guide to YPOs* at ypsuccess.com

For example, I recently added to my network a gentleman whom I met at a local coffee shop. I was running in to get a caffeine boost, and I walked by a table where a man sat reading a business book. I asked him if he thought it was a worthwhile book to read. He had just started reading it and had not formed an opinion yet. I asked him if he wouldn't mind shooting me an e-mail when he was finished. I gave him a business card and suggested that he use it as his new bookmark.

I knew it was a coin flip: would I ever hear from the man again? Yes. About two weeks later I received an e-mail. He talked about the book and asked about my work, based on the information on my business card.

I scrolled to the bottom of his e-mail to learn he was vice president of human resources at a major corporation. It was not hard to surmise why he was interested in a young professional's leadership development and training experience. This is an unusual and rare example of success in completely random networking, but it does show the value of continually pursuing a larger network.

The second and more traditional way of building your network is through established networking channels. These include chambers of commerce, industry organizations, alumni associations, and young professional groups. Most of these organizations focus largely on networking and building relationships among members, so it's not hard to see the logic there.

However, other organizations not created specifically for networking also provide a great venue. Would you be surprised to learn that networking is a major reason why people may be involved in a nonprofit organization or a church? Remember, networking can be used as a tool for personal growth (meeting like-minded people at your church), not only for career growth—but the two aren't necessarily mutually exclusive.

BUILDING AND GROWING YOUR RELATIONSHIPS
So you made the handshake, exchanged names, and found out what organizations each of you work for and what you do for your respective companies. Now what do you talk about?

As you have undoubtedly noticed, a lot of these chapters offer intertwining concepts—and here is an opportunity to bring back

Soak It Up! and pre-call planning. If you were planning ahead for a specific event, you would have some questions ready to go, topics that would keep the conversation flowing. If you are new to an organization and do not know the attendees, some "stock" questions that can get things going are "How long have you been involved in this organization?" or "What part of this organization have you found particularly valuable?"

Keep up with current events in the national news, the local business journal, and any relevant industry blogs; you can usually relate some news item to any industry with a whole host of questions along the lines of "How do you think that will affect your industry?" If the person has not read a particular article, this is an opportunity to talk about it briefly—and thus provide value.

Don't forget: the most important part of asking questions is to actually listen and pay attention to the answers! You can only build and grow relationships by actually caring and learning about one another.

While I was doing some marketing work for an organization and staying at a hotel in Minneapolis, I enjoyed a drink at the hotel bar (often a great spot for networking!). There happened to be a union conference for bus drivers at this same hotel. Some of the bus drivers tried to strike up conversations with members of our group, but our group was less than friendly, and I think I knew why. The individuals I was with were probably earning three to four times the amount of money the bus drivers made. It was apparent that they felt their financial and job status put them in a different social category.

Once again, ego becomes a problem here, and we know by now that an outsized ego is no good to anyone. Not only that, but if you hang around people who are just like you all the time, how will you learn something new? How will you get a better understanding of how other people live? Remember, information is crucial to success, in both life and work. Plus, sometimes talking to others can be a motivating or even life-changing experience. You can have more fun than you ever imagined talking with people from different walks of life.

Our group ended up leaving the hotel to go out to dinner, but I stayed back and ordered hotel bar food. I had a great time with the bus drivers that evening, particularly James from the Texas Panhandle and Carlos from California. Good beer and great conversation made for a fun and interesting evening!

Ryan Emerson
Special Projects Manager
PRICEWATERHOUSECOOPERS

Our future is influenced by the leadership of today and tomorrow.

Several years ago I was an intern at a congressional office in Washington, D.C. I sat at the front desk and had the difficult—sometimes confrontational—duty of screening phone callers and office visitors. Several times a day various lobbyists would come into the office building to see the congressman, or at least the legislative assistant. There were several I knew never to let in, several to let in always, and then a remaining percentage with whom I could exercise my judgment.

I will never forget one of the lobbyists: he was published, and he clearly had money, power, and a network of connections in the most powerful city in the world. He was well mannered in every observable way. But what distinguished him from nearly every other lobbyist was his disposition toward me. The first time he entered the office, he took time to learn my name, my wife's name, where I was from, and where I was going. He asked about these things with sincerity, and I believed he really wanted to know about me. From that time forward, we were friendly. When we would meet, he always called me by name, asked (by name) how my wife was doing, and asked how my applications to graduate school were progressing—he even offered to help. I looked forward to his visits, and I always ensured that he was treated well.

Fast-forward two years: I returned to work for the congressman as a legislative assistant. Now I was the one meeting with lobbyists and—if I felt inclined—inviting the congressman to join us. Guess who got star treatment? I remembered every one of those lobbyists from my internship, and I rarely met with any of them. But my friend was always welcome, and he met with the congressman at his request.

So many times young professionals trip over themselves to impress the boss, often to the extent of alienating their coworkers. We should always remember that our future is influenced by the leadership of today and tomorrow.

When you begin to attend networking events in order to create and expand your network, you will most likely encounter four types of people.

The first is the Salesman. It is obvious that this person is there to make a sale, and everyone in that room is nothing more than a prospect for a sale. The Salesman is not interested in anything you do or say—unless you are interested in his product or service.

The second type is the Wandering Eye. This is my least favorite type. Have you ever started talking to someone who has already begun looking for the next person, with wandering eyes? This person is clearly seeking someone more important than you. At least the Salesman has potential; this person may be a lost cause.

The third type of person is the Business Card Grabber. This person is a combination of the Salesman and the Wandering Eye, but is not necessarily a bad person. The Grabber is too focused on quantity and fails to consider the all-important quality of the relationship. This person is all about making as many connections as possible.

There is one other type of person out there, thankfully; he or she is Someone of Value. This is someone who understands what I talked about earlier—that a relationship is about providing mutual value to each other. This Someone of Value has the ability to hold a real conversation and can establish a connection with you. This person provides value to you either personally or professionally through his experiences and knowledge (in which case he is a potential mentor).

Being Someone of Value can be challenging when you focus on the wrong goals in networking. Early in my career, I could have fit into the category of Salesman, Wandering Eye, or Business Card Grabber. I have learned from my mistakes and can now consider myself Someone of Value! It is definitely a process and a lifelong journey.

Edward K. Aldag, Jr.
Chairman, President & CEO
MEDICAL PROPERTIES TRUST, INC.

I started Medical Properties Trust, Inc., in 2003. The idea for the company came to me in 2002 after a nearly twenty-year history in the workforce. What MPT does and what type of business it is in is totally irrelevant to the lesson behind the story of this start-up. For anyone starting out in any industry, there are three main things that are worth learning from my experience in starting MPT.

1. **Believe**. I learned early on in my business life (and quite frankly, it probably holds true in almost every part of your life) that if you don't enjoy or believe in what you do, you'd better find something else to do. When I came up with the idea of MPT, it was the culmination of almost twenty years of work experiences. It was an idea that I believed in. When you truly believe in something, people can tell.

   When I started this company, we had no assets; it was just me and an idea. The first thing I had to do was to put together a founding team. In order to do this, the people I was trying to convince to join me had to know I believed in what I was doing. When you believe in something, no one can sell the idea like you can. If you don't believe in what you are selling, no one will buy it.

   Over the next six months I put together a team of three other gentlemen and myself. At this point, I wasn't paying anyone; we didn't have any money. But they all knew that I believed, and they believed. On to the next step.

2. **Never give up**. A few months after MPT got listed on the NYSE, my father visited me in my office and asked, "Ed, how did you pull this off?" After a few seconds of thinking about a question I had never really pondered, I answered, "Dad, I guess I was just too stupid to know when to quit!" After much more reflection, I found that there was a tremendous amount of truth in that quick answer to my father. I had an idea that I truly believed in—an idea that I knew was needed and would work. I had convinced three other bright men to join me without pay. We

knew this was a great idea that was going to generate great investor returns and create untold opportunities in the health care industry in communities all over the country.

We had numerous devastating setbacks along the way. But as I look back on those days, there was never a time when we said, "Well, it's over." Even with each setback and each "no" I received on the venture capital circuit, we kept pushing. We never gave up!

If you truly believe in something, don't give up—keep pushing. There will be plenty of no's along your path to success.

3. **The world is small**. How you treat people today will matter twenty years later. My very first transaction with MPT involved a gentleman with whom I had done business twenty years before. We'd had a great relationship back then, and I remembered him as a straight shooter who was easy to work with and whose word was his bond. We both made sure we did what we said we would do. And eventually we went our separate ways, most likely never to see each other again.

Fast-forward twenty years, and our paths crossed again—mine with MPT and his with a start-up company needing funding. MPT and his company ended up doing the largest transaction together in both companies' history. Remember, the world is small—everything comes back, so be sure to deal with others as you would be dealt with!

In fact, most life lessons stem from making mistakes and persevering. You heard about my exploding ego in "Don't Believe the Hype," and there was definitely a time in my life when major blunders—being too proud, failing to stimulate my colleagues through work, getting too big for my britches—threatened my career progress. But today's mistakes will be remembered tomorrow as valuable experience. The point is, building relationships is an important skill that can be learned over time.

I was fortunate to know a great relationship builder in my own father. My dad has a lot of admirable qualities, but there is one in particular that I hope to emulate: his ability to make the person at the other end of the conversation feel at ease, whether it's the janitor or the CEO. My dad is comfortable connecting with anybody from any walk of life.

> *"Growing up, I saw that my dad did not need to brag or boast—and that has stuck with me."*

The secret is he has no secret. That's simply who he is. So my question was, what made him like this? What can I do to acquire that skill, to really care about people from all walks of life? What in my dad's personality made those conversations come naturally? I realized the key is that he sees every person as equal. He doesn't care about what car a person drives or whether that person has a Rolex.

My dad grew up with great values, worked his way through college, and rose through the ranks of his company. At one time in his career, he had an office in four different cities on the West Coast, and we lived in a high-end gated community in California. I remember my dad striking up a conversation with a repairman at our house. I heard the repairman ask, "Sir, you have a beautiful home here. Can I ask what you do for a living?" My dad replied, "I peddle light bulbs." (He worked in sales for a major lighting company.) The gentleman was taken aback. Most people would have used the opportunity to use their title or position, but that wasn't my dad.

Growing up, I saw that my dad did not need to brag or boast—and that has stuck with me. He was comfortable with who he was, and he didn't feel the need to impress. Because of this, building relationships came naturally to him.

MAINTAINING YOUR RELATIONSHIPS

This generation has no excuse for not maintaining relationships. Our parents' generation had to rely on face-to-face communication, the landline telephone, and snail mail. We now have e-mail, text messaging, mobile phones, Facebook, Twitter, instant messenges, and myriad other forms of communication and social networking. With all this practice and all these opportunities, we should all be masters at maintaining relationships.

There is no real science to maintaining relationships, other than time and effort.

E-mail is the greatest tool for maintaining relationships that most people have in their arsenal. For example, if I read a great article in the *San Antonio Business Journal* on commercial real estate, I'll send it in an e-mail to a friend who works in the industry. This provides value to our relationship. Or if you have not heard from someone for a period of time, it is easy to shoot him or her an e-mail saying, "How are things going? Anything new at XYZ Company?"

However, e-mail communication can become dangerous because it is impersonal. E-mail is a great way to stay in touch, but face-to-face interaction or phone calls are crucial to building and maintaining relationships. Any opportunity that presents itself can be a reason to call for a chat or to meet for lunch or coffee; this is where you build relationships. E-mail is great for staying in touch and maintaining, but personal interaction is better for growing a relationship.

My favorite and most effective form of maintaining relationships is through handwritten notes. Think about this: How many e-mails or text messages do you get every day? How many hand-written notes do you get every day? While e-mail is much easier and faster than a handwritten note, the impact of saying thank you in writing is incomparable. People remember a handwritten note. It is personal, and people truly appreciate that. Making the extra effort to write a note shows someone that you value him or her—that you value your relationship.

The next time you meet someone new, try making this effort. Send a note that says, "It was a pleasure meeting you the other day at the chamber luncheon. Here is my business card—let's stay in touch." To further personalize the note, throw in a line about a specific conversation you had or mention something about the event you attended. The notes that I write are usually only three to four sentences.

In addition, always handwrite your thank-you notes. This is becoming a lost art, so with that simple act you can differentiate yourself from the crowd. When I give a talk to a college

> "*Making the extra effort to write a note shows someone that you value him or her.*"

or a young professional group, I almost always receive thank-you e-mails, but only occasionally do I get a handwritten thank-you note. E-mails are nice, but a written thank-you will stand out in the recipient's memory!

Above all, in striving to maintain your relationships, remember that providing mutual value is of primary importance. When it comes down to it, the medium you choose for keeping in touch won't matter if your communication is not sincere and productive. If you are not someone who provides value to the people in your network, you may gradually lose touch and ultimately end up destroying the relationship.

Tom Darrow

Founder & Principal, TALENT CONNECTIONS, LLC
Founder & Principal, CAREER SPA, LLC

Every day, do things to cultivate your existing network and build on it.

When I started my business in 1999, I was having breakfast with a mentor of mine. He asked me, "What do you think is the most important aspect of your business?" I replied, "My expertise." He replied, "Wrong—it is your network."

He was right! Over the years, it has been clear that having a deep network has been critical to selling our services. Most people think networking is passing out business cards. Not so! Networking is about being connected with others in a trusting, mutually value-added relationship.

> Tom recommends *The Customer Comes Second,* by Hal Rosenbluth

So how does one accomplish this? Find ways to bring value to others. Volunteer. Speak. Write articles. Give away tickets. Connect people to one another. Teach. Build things with others. Don't be afraid to fail. Be genuine. Give more than you receive.

In the end, what you give out will be returned in multiples. Don't just collect business cards; build a fan club!

CALLING ON YOUR NETWORK

If you have gone through the work of building and maintaining a network, you need to get something out of it, right?

Calling on your network is the simple act of reaching out to individuals for specific needs. As president of Young Execs of San Antonio, I became friends with the general manager of an upscale restaurant in town. When I was involved in a nonprofit fundraiser gala and was asked to see if I could help get silent auction items donated, I called my friend, who was happy to give us a gift certificate from her restaurant. That is calling on your network.

Even in a more self-serving situation, such as trying to get a meeting with a director or manager at a specific company, you may know someone in your network who is friends with that person. Use that network; make a phone call and ask for assistance in setting up that meeting.

These are just two examples of capitalizing on the benefits of your network. I find that, in reality, I use my network several times a week, for a variety of reasons. But remember, the key to a great personal network is to continually provide value to the members in it. So if you continue to ask for things without giving back, the network will become smaller and less likely to help when you need it. Look actively for ways to provide value to your network—this could mean referring business, providing business intelligence on competitors, or even simply sending an e-mail with a link to a great magazine article about someone's industry.

Your network will be invaluable to you in the progression of your career. It could be the key to your next job, your next big client, or your future partner in your first big business venture.

M. Cass Wheeler
Strategic Consultant, Coach, and Speaker
Former CEO, AMERICAN HEART ASSOCIATION

It's not enough to have "hard skills," like analytical abilities; you must have "soft skills," too.

Soft skills are getting along well with others in a variety of situations, building strong relationships, and establishing trust. You have to make deposits in other people's emotional bank accounts before you can make withdrawals.

Skillfully using soft resources such as trust will help move hard resources (dollars and people).

Cass recommends his book called: *You've Gotta Have Heart*

One final thought about the art of conversation and networking comes from a luncheon I recently attended. It was a typical industry-organization luncheon with a speaker, networking opportunities, door prizes, and nametags. The topic or the speaker is typically what brings me to luncheons like this, but of course networking is an added benefit. In fact, every time I am out, I use the opportunity to network, establish relationships, and prospect for clients.

I sat down at a table and introduced myself to everyone. The two attendees sitting on my right were from the same company, and the two attendees on my left also were from the same respective company. So I'd already found one problem at this table: people from the same company were sitting together. If your job requires you to attend luncheons (either internal luncheons or events with a variety of people attending), my advice is, don't just sit with people you know. Most salespeople know this because they cannot prospect for clients when they are surrounded by coworkers. However, every person can benefit from sitting next to someone you do not already know.

After introducing myself, I sat down hoping to join in on the conversation that was taking place. However, there was no conversation. There were four people sitting at a table, just watching as people walked about mingling in the dining hall.

So I began asking questions. The young professionals at the table answered the questions as simply as they could. Two of them worked for a marketing firm, and the other two worked for an engineering firm. They gave no elaboration on their job roles, showed no excitement about the lunch today, and asked no questions about who I was or what I did.

An older gentleman soon sat at our table and introduced himself, but our tablemates just nodded and continued to stare into space. I began talking to the man and learned he had recently retired from the American Red Cross and had been in communications and public relations. He worked specifically on the American Red Cross's public relations for major disasters: hurricanes, earthquakes, floods, etc.

Naturally, hundreds of questions came to mind.

As I spoke with this interesting gentleman, I looked around our table and noticed a continued lack of interest. I was taken aback. How could these people not take an interest in making conversation with someone who'd had such an interesting career and experiences?

Relationships are at the core of everything, in business and in life. If you enjoy a conversation or show interest in people, it can help you on the road to success—not to mention keeping you entertained along the way.

So get out there and build relationships, and grow your network. You will be glad you did, especially when you have a need to call on someone. And maybe one day you will have created so many fans and built such a large network that people will begin knowing who you are without you even knowing them.

Jeffrey Berding
Director of Sales & Public Affairs
CINCINNATI BENGALS

In an interview, I asked a candidate what appealed to him about the job, and he was honest: "Meeting the players and having the chance to become friends with them." The interview ended shortly thereafter, and no offer was made. Clearly, the focus was not on doing the job.

Focus on the job at hand.

A game-day intern, whose responsibilities were in the Club Lounge, was witnessed in the stadium tunnel outside our home locker room. He was encouraging players as they made their way to the field for the game. His internship ended after the game. The focus was not on doing his job.

Another intern was down on the field for pregame warm-ups, taking photos of the players and asking for autographs. His internship ended. The focus was not on doing the job.

Given that many of our junior staff started out with internships, these individuals missed out on possible future paid opportunities with the team. My advice? Focus on the job at hand, and you may find that more important jobs will come your way. One thing is certain: if you don't focus, those jobs will never come along.

ATTITUDE, CONFIDENCE, AND PASSION

Companies are hiring for attitude and training for skill.

12

Emmett D. Carson, PhD

President & CEO

SILICON VALLEY COMMUNITY FOUNDATION

In a global economy in which jobs will be increasingly competitive, soft skills—e.g., demeanor, attitude, and customer service orientation—will prove to be the secret edge for motivated job seekers.

Intertwined with all the discussions of personal development that I've shared with you throughout this book are several prevailing traits: attitude, confidence, and passion. You must cultivate these aspects of your personality, because they could hold the key to finding a job or to your success in the workplace.

Most of the managers or business owners I know have adopted the approach of "hire for attitude, train for skill." With technology improving the processes in just about every area, the specific skills that were once in high demand among employers (accounting, information technology, etc.) may become obsolete in the future. Who knows what jobs will be available in five or ten years? The job market may not be in need of your specific skill set anymore.

However, your "soft skills"—such as relationship building, teamwork, attitude, and leadership—often will be what differentiate you from other workers. We may not know what skills are needed for the future, but I can guarantee that a great attitude and strong leadership will always have a place in any organization.

Jeff Ittel

Senior Vice President, Semiconductor Business Group
AVNET, INC.

I have been in the electronics distribution business for twenty-one years and have held just about every position in sales, sales management, product marketing, and operations at Avnet, Inc., a $10 billion-plus company. I am currently responsible for the semiconductor business in the Americas.

One story I would like to share actually happened to me many years ago when I was an account manager in Los Angeles. I have shared this story many times with new employees at Avnet.

The semiconductor business is very cyclical. There are boom periods, where demand is great and your results are limited only by how much product you can find for your customer. Then there are bust periods, where the industry is over-supplied and you have to fight the competition for every order, then just hope you made some money on the order.

These bust times, or "buyer's markets," are especially tough on distribution. Distributors don't make any product. Oftentimes, competition sells the same types of products, even the same OEM (original equipment manufacturer) lines. We were in a brutal buyer's market in the late 1980s.

I had one client (a division of TRW) who actually had some nice contracts coming in, and as a result, the purchasing department was being bombarded by every salesman in the Los Angeles Basin. I had made several proposals and sales calls, and it was coming down to decision time on some very high-priced devices that would be used on this project. I made my final sales call on the account, feeling very anxious and nervous, as a portion of this order would go a long way in rectifying an otherwise tough summer of selling.

On the call, little time was spent reviewing the final numbers. The numbers had been turned and were well understood. It was a beautiful day, and for some reason I was in a great mood, despite my current lack of sales for the month. In conversations with the buyer, a lot of discussion took place on topics other than the order of the day. We took care of other business and spent some time making small talk, even laughing a bit on a few shared stories.

The buyer was more than fifty years old; I was in my mid-twenties. So he had a lot more experience than I did, and I figured that taking the "hard sell" route would not do me a lot of good anyway.

The buyer told me he would make his decision the following day. As I left the office, several of my competitors were in the waiting area, waiting for their turn at a final pitch for the business. I thought to myself, "I may have not given this my best effort." I felt that I really hadn't laid it on the line.

Later that day I received a call from the buyer. He told me that not only was I going to get a portion of the order, I was going to get the entire order. I could not believe it. As I thanked him, he told me something that I will never forget. He said, "Jeff, you are not getting this order because of the price or the company you work for. You are getting it because of your attitude. I have seen every salesman in town today, and you are the only one who didn't come in here begging or playing me, asking for sympathy on how tough it is out there and how bad you need the order. You actually had a smile on your face, and it was the only pleasurable meeting I had all day."

The lesson I took from this was very basic and simple: people want to do business with people they like, with people they believe are successful. I truly believe that everyone wants to associate themselves with others who are confident and are enjoying life. Take the

> You can't control market conditions, but you can control your attitude.

time to let your true personality show through. Take the time to smile and be friendly. When you are doing this and your competition isn't, you will win more times than not.

That day many years ago in Los Angeles, I could not control the market conditions that I was working in. But I could control my own attitude. And attitude should not be underestimated.

Passion sells. A positive, passionate attitude will sell you to an employer. It will sell your product to a prospect. It will sell an idea to your manager. When you are passionate about something, your body language changes and you exude excitement. You exude confidence, and people are drawn to that.

Are you passionate about what you currently doing? Are you passionate about some parts of your job but not others? Try to find ways to spend more time doing what you are passionate about, and less time on what you are not. Those things that you are passionate about and spend more time on will be the projects that build your career.

> "*Find ways to spend more time doing what you are passionate about.*"

Your first few years of work are critical to establishing your personal brand and your resume. If your goal is to be a CEO or upper management, but you do not like your current job or company, it will be extremely challenging to move up the ranks. Your dissatisfaction will be evident to your organization; your heart will not be in it, and your performance will not be as great. However, if you are passionate about what you do, your organization will notice this and will want you to succeed and move up through the ranks. You must be passionate about what you currently do in order to achieve career momentum.

Jeannine M. Rivet
Executive Vice President
UNITEDHEALTH GROUP

Life gives back what you give it.

Know your strengths, and build upon them. People always enjoy doing what is most comfortable and natural to them; for example, do not try to be a financial expert if your strength is in sales. However, discover how to supplement your strengths with learned skills, and identify resources that can help you complement your talents.

Jeannine recommends *QBQ! The Question Behind the Question,* by John G. Miller.

Life is a journey of continuous learning and development. Every experience, particularly during difficult or unpleasant times in your life or career, creates an opportunity to grow. Be true to yourself, and enjoy all aspects of your life. Create your own echo, as I learned from the following story.

A young boy and his father were walking in the mountains. Suddenly the boy falls, hurts himself, and screams! To his surprise, he hears the scream repeating somewhere in the mountain.

Curious, he yells, "Who are you?"

He receives the answer: "Who are you?"

Confused by the response, he screams, "Coward!"

He hears this repeated to him: "Coward!"

So he looks to his father and asks, "What's going on?"

The father smiles and says, "My son, pay attention."

And then he screams to the mountain, "I admire you!"

The voice answers, "I admire you!"

The man then screams, "You are a champion!"

The voice answers, "You are a champion!"

The boy is surprised but does not understand.

Like an echo, life gives back everything you say and do.

Then the father explains: "People call this an echo, but really this is life. It gives back everything you say or do. Our life is simply a reflection of our actions."

So if you want more love in the world, create more love in your heart. If you want more competence in your team, improve your own competence. This relationship applies to everything, in all aspects of life. Life will give you back everything you have given to it.

Your passion can also be for what your organization does. I know plenty of people who do not have a high level of passion for their specific job, but they are passionate about the organization they work for. This is more of a realistic expectation for a young professional, since you probably will not be starting your career with the position of your dreams, much less with a secretary and the plush corner office. But if you believe in the organization and its purpose, success will follow.

If you find yourself in a job or setting that doesn't inspire your passion, do yourself and your organization a favor—find a new job. And hurry—before you become a paycheck player.

Kevin Lee
Cofounder, Chairman & CEO
DIDIT

Passion combines with intelligence and dedication to assure success. For both my career and the careers of the young employees I hire, a common thread is passion.

These young professionals may not enter my company feeling passionate about our business or about helping clients. However, they soon deploy their innate passion toward the Didit mission, and they become passionate about helping clients maximize their profit from paid search and online marketing. That passion is a necessary component of our team's attitude and approach, and it also becomes a stimulus for progression, learning, and growth. Raises and promotions follow in a natural course.

During our working years, we all spend the bulk of our waking hours involved in our career. That makes it even more important that we love what we do. Passion makes a career less like work and more rewarding psychologically. Money can motivate only to a certain threshold. It takes love of one's place in a business or social ecosystem to provide overall fulfillment.

In high school, I was not the best baseball player on the team, but I worked hard and gained my coaches' respect. On my first sales team, I was not the best salesperson, but again I worked very hard and gained my manager's respect.

I learned early on that by working hard, strangely enough, you may actually alienate some of your teammates as opposed to gaining their admiration. I'm not sure whether this is caused by jealousy, their own guilt for not working hard, or another reason. But I've worked with plenty of business teams and played on sports teams that had a "Negative Nellie," and I know there are a lot of these types of people around, looking to bring you down.

> "*Negative people feed off of the negativity of others and the reassurance that their feelings are shared.*"

You may know who I am speaking about. The guy who makes the smart-aleck comments to make you feel guilty about working hard or cooperating with authority figures: "You've got some brown stuff on your nose." Or the girl who makes assumptions and spreads rumors about your promotion being a result of your good looks, not your work. There are always going to be people who want to antagonize you and keep you from succeeding. This is an unavoidable truth in both business and life.

The challenge is to press on, keep a positive attitude, and be confident in what you do. When someone is negative, keep sharing the positives. Negative people feed off of the negativity of others and the reassurance that their feelings are shared. If you do not feed their negativity, it will eventually starve and die! Positive energy, passion, and pride can help you establish practices that will put you ahead of the pack. In some cases, it can raise you up from the most difficult circumstances to the top of the heap.

Philip C. S. Yin, PhD
Chairman & CEO
AXT INC.

I am the son of the former consulate general of the Soviet Union (1941–1949), who was stationed at the Chinese Consulate in Al-Ma-Ta. My father represented the Chinese National Government (Kuomintang), which at the time was led by General Chiang Kai-shek.

As you know from history, after the communist takeover of China led by Mao Tse-tung, the communist Soviet Union no longer recognized the Chinese National Government. We were provided with three months of diplomatic immunity, after which we were to leave the country...or be arrested!

My father wanted my older brother and me to obtain the best education possible, and thus he chose the United States as the place we would settle down. From this day on, our entire lifestyle changed dramatically. My brother and I did not read, write, or speak English.

My father purchased a chicken farm in Lakewood, New Jersey, and my mother was able to find work in a clock factory assembling clocks for seventy-five cents per hour. Up to this point in our lives, we'd had a chauffeur, a maid, two cooks, a gardener, and a nanny. My mother did not even know how to cook rice.

I was nine years old and was able to obtain a job washing dishes in the local Chinese restaurant Friday through Sunday for $5 per day. I eventually moved up to waiter and second cook as I worked at the restaurant through high school.

In college, I majored in physics. Upon graduation I was drafted by the Army, but I chose to join the Marine Corps instead, knowing that I was most likely to be sent to Vietnam and thus wanted to be trained to be the best. After being in combat for eight months and twenty-two days, I was wounded and eventually came back stateside to Camp Lejeune. After my discharge, I was able to secure employment with a chemical company, and then in 1969 was recruited by IBM's Thomas J. Watson Research Center, where I worked as a research associate.

I eventually received my doctorate in physics, left IBM, and worked for various companies in both manufacturing and sales. With Monsanto, I basically opened up the markets in the People's Republic of China and Taiwan for silicon substrates for IC applications.

My career continued progressing, and I held my first high-level position as vice president of sales and marketing for Kawatec (owned by Kawasaki Steel Corporation). I then held high-level positions with both Mitsubishi Silicon America and Crysteco. After five years of quadrupling sales revenues at Crysteco, the company went bankrupt due to embezzlement by the venture capital partners. I was given two days' notice to pack my personal belongings and vacate my office!

Here I was with a wife and a brand-new house—and with no job for the first time in my life! Fortunately, the next day I received a phone call from an old friend with whom I kept in touch while I was at IBM and Monsanto. He offered me a job as president of ATMI, Epitaxial Division. After three years of helping increase sales revenues and the stock price, I decided to form my own consulting firm. After only two years of self-employment, however, I was recruited to my current position as CEO of AXT.

Through all of my years of various positions at different companies, I have learned a great deal. To understand my managing philosophy, I feel it is important to know about my background. In a nutshell, I have modified Jack Welch's approach to managing. I call it the 5 Es and 2 Ps:

1. ENERGY
2. ENERGIZE
3. EFFECTIVENESS
4. EDGE
5. EMOTIONAL INTELLIGENCE
6. PASSION
7. PRIDE

My other important management recommendation for up-and-coming executives is to treat everyone as you would like to be treated. Never think that you are above other people. Always put yourself in their shoes before you respond or react! I always remind our employees (all 928 of them) that I am no different from them; I put my pants on the same way every day, as they do. My office door is always open to anyone who needs to speak with me for whatever reason or issue, whether it is personal or company related.

I also remind the professional employees (especially the executives and high-level managers) that I am a "hands-off" manager. The reason those managers were recruited is that they know more about a particular area of responsibility than I do. Thus, I will never be looking over their shoulder—unless it's because they need assistance.

My recruitment philosophy is to hire people who know more than me; that way, I can learn from them. Never feel threatened, or you will never have an effective staff.

Last, but not least, every year at the Christmas party I remind all the employees that human capital is our greatest asset, by telling them, "You, the employees, are the core of the company."

We as executives and managers provide the plans, resources, etc. However, it is the employees who need to execute to make things happen successfully. Without the dedicated efforts of all the employees, a company will never achieve its goals and objectives.

In fact, I instruct that the quarterly MBO (management by objectives) results of all executives (including me) are to be posted on the bulletin board at corporate headquarters; they also are translated into Chinese and posted at the manufacturing facility in China. Thus, everyone can see how well or how poorly each executive performed during the quarter. My philosophy is that are no unnecessary secrets between management and the employees. The more the employees know about what is going on within the company, the more they feel that they are part of the company, working as a team to successfully execute each and every one of their specific responsibilities.

A great example of an always positive attitude comes from a friend of mine—I'll call him Jim. Jim had a coworker who constantly complained about their boss. The coworker expressed his opinion that their manager was horrible and claimed that this caused his lack of motivation to work.

I knew that Jim was not fond of his boss, either, but he kept his negative feelings from his colleagues.

One day, Jim's coworker came to him and said, "Jim, why do you work so hard for our boss? Can't you see that all you're doing is making our boss look better? He'll never get fired."

Jim smiled and said, "You may be right. But as long as I do my job well, I won't get fired. And if we all make our boss look really good, he'll get promoted—and we won't have to deal with him anymore." Talk about finding a silver lining! In Jim's view, the only way to succeed in this situation was to take the high road—and he did. This way, he avoided the stress of a negative attitude, and focused on his passion for the work, confident of better times ahead.

Now, presuming they have equal skills, who do you think is more likely to succeed in his career: Jim or his coworker?

Ben Kirchhoff
Young Entrepreneur

Once you begin working on a new business venture, do not be discouraged by adversity at any stage of development. Even if it feels as though you're going nowhere, you are absorbing knowledge and experience by continuing to research and develop your ideas further. Opportunities come when you least expect them, and being prepared will be your best weapon to land that golden opportunity.

When I decided to start my first business, in college, I thought it was the best idea in the world and could not believe no one had thought of it before.

My thinking went straight to "How can I charge for this service?" and not "How will this service benefit others?" I was going ninety miles per hour with no direction, and I quickly learned that although I was excited and could not wait to get started, I needed a lot of help.

After figuring out the areas in which I needed help, I soon found a team of people to both give me advice and help me develop my idea even further. My business was starting to take shape, and I made sure I learned as much as possible about the market I was trying to enter.

Before I knew it, I crossed paths with the CEO of a software company who was impressed enough with my hard work and dedication that he helped me come into contact with people I would never have had the opportunity to talk with otherwise. Being prepared to talk about my ideas and business with confidence helped open the door to new opportunities.

BE SELFISH AND VOLUNTEER

Volunteering for a nonprofit organization doesn't have to be a totally selfless act—you can benefit, too.

13

I've always wondered why, when someone tries to humble someone else, one of the first clichés to be brought out is "The world doesn't revolve around you." I do understand the intent of the adage—people should not be so self-centered that they fail to see that other people exist—but in all honesty, my world does revolve around me. I do not know what my friends or colleagues are doing when I am not around them. I do not know what is happening in Italy or China if I am not there. Of course, I could watch a news report about what's affecting people in Italy or China, or I could call up a friend and find out what's going on "in his world." But in fact, we each have our own little world that does revolve around us, because what we see and what we do is all that we know.

I explained this in an introduction to a speech I gave to a group of college students, and then continued to have a lot of fun with the concept throughout the speech. My challenge to all these students was to be selfish and volunteer for a nonprofit. Yes, I said "selfish," not "selfless." I went a bit to the extreme with my approach to encouraging these college students to volunteer. After all, what better way to encourage volunteerism than to prove to young people in a "What's in it for me?" society that they can benefit from this practice.

One of the ways you can benefit from volunteering for a nonprofit is by sharpening your skills. Let's say that you want to pursue a marketing career, and you've prepared yourself thus far by completing a marketing degree. Your current employment is in market research, however, and this is not allowing you to work on your creative skills or engage your marketing interests. A volunteer role with a nonprofit is a prime opportunity to hone your talents and develop your passion for marketing. Offer to help promote and market the nonprofit, and not only will you be able to sharpen and improve your marketing skills, but you will also have a case study and experience to add to your resume.

Find yourself still asking, "What's in it for me?" Although I cannot guarantee anything, I know from experience that a number of perks can come out of volunteering for a nonprofit. These can range from free meals (some organizations have board and committee meetings at restaurants, or host dinner meetings at their offices) to a fully paid trip to another city.

I remember one perk in particular. I was an avid volunteer with the South Texas chapter of Junior Achievement from 2000 to 2004, and a big promoter of the organization among my fellow Young Execs members and friends. (An organization like Junior Achievement is a great starting point for first-time volunteers; it is simple, extremely organized, and requires only one to two hours per week for around seven weeks.) While I was volunteering, I got a phone call from one of the Junior Achievement staff members inviting me to play in a fundraising golf tournament as a guest of a sponsor. The corporate sponsor had apparently bought a foursome at this golf tournament every year, to be filled by dedicated Junior Achievement volunteers. Because of my volunteering and the relationships I had established with the Junior Achievement staff, I was able to play in a golf tournament that otherwise would have cost me $675.

Visit www.ja.org for more information.

Another extremely valuable benefit you may receive from volunteering for a nonprofit is the contacts that you will make. Have you ever read a CEO's bio or heard someone introduce a high-level executive at an event? More than likely, the resumes of these individuals include "chairman of XYZ Nonprofit Organization" and "director on the board of Good Deeds Association." Some CEOs take a more active role within a nonprofit, and some take the role strictly on an honorary basis.

The relationships you make while volunteering will go beyond meeting a specific CEO or community leader. You will meet many people from all different walks of life, with different occupations, industries, backgrounds, and educations. Your network will become more diverse, and no longer will everyone you meet through an industry association work in the same field.

So remember, there are freebies to be had and particular benefits to you as an individual for volunteering for a nonprofit. However, the best reason to volunteer is because of the benefit you can provide to the organization and the feeling you will get while doing so. Find an organization that you are passionate about and that you truly want to help. If you do that, then you actually won't care if you receive a free meal or a round of golf—the satisfaction of working and giving to the organization will be the best freebie you get.

David Williams
President & CEO
MAKE-A-WISH FOUNDATION OF AMERICA

"Everybody can be great because anybody can serve. You don't have to have a college degree to serve. You don't have to make your subject and verb agree to serve. You only need a heart full of grace—a soul generated by love."

— Martin Luther King Jr.

The year was 1981, and I was a recent college graduate and freshly minted accountant with the Shell Oil Company. During that year, I began volunteering with Big Brothers & Big Sisters, with Bread for the World, and at my church. But I had not really found my niche in my volunteer activities.

One Saturday, while attending an all-day session on the issue of world hunger, a presentation was made about a fledgling nonprofit organization called the Houston-Galveston Area Food Bank. It was about six months old and had experienced a very rough start. The executive director invited me for a tour of the facility and asked me to join their fundraising committee.

I soon found myself making presentations to potential donors and enjoying it immensely. Because of my accounting background, I was asked to become the treasurer and to join the board of directors. In less than two months, the executive director resigned and I was asked to take on this full-time position.

While I was at the Food Bank, another nonprofit organization was getting started in Houston: Habitat for Humanity. The Houston affiliate needed a place to store building supplies, and the Food Bank provided that space at no cost. This initiated my long volunteer experience with Habitat for Humanity.

In 1994, I left the Food Bank to become the COO of Habitat for Humanity International, headquartered in Georgia. So, in retrospect, volunteering with nonprofits twice led me to make significant changes in my life and profession.

I became involved with nonprofit organizations as a means to live out my Christian faith. Working with and on behalf of those in need of decent shelter or a meal, or for children with life-threatening illnesses has been incredibly rewarding. I have also had the opportunity to work with caring and gifted people who want to make a difference in the world.

I would recommend to any young professional that you volunteer your time to a cause for which you have a passion—to a mission that "melts your butter." You will learn a great deal about yourself. You will meet smart and passionate people. And you will have an opportunity to be salt and light in a hurting and dark world.

Joseph D. Roman
President & CEO
GREATER CLEVELAND PARTNERSHIP

The world revolves around politics, in government and in business. However, the experiences and dynamics in each are vastly different.

I believe that one of the most valuable experiences any young person can get is experience in Washington, D.C. Anything from a three- or four-month internship to a couple of years on Capitol Hill as a staffer for anyone—elected official or not—will fit the bill. I did it many years ago, and I find myself regularly benefiting from knowing a little bit more about the insides of decision making in the political arena. Trust me, understanding the world of governmental politics will give you a big leg up in the corporate political world. And you will also enjoy it.

Someday, after a successful career, making that decision to run for office will also be a little easier!

GENERATION ADDvice

14

Leaders and executives contribute advice in a format perfect for our A.D.D. generation.

The first chapter, "Generation A.D.D.," explained some of the challenges that young professionals face as a result of our ever-shortening attention spans. In this chapter, executives kindly give their advice in a format that is conducive to our generation's desire for information in a short-and-sweet package.

Richard A. Bross

President

HORMEL FOODS INTERNATIONAL CORPORATION

Here goes—a long-standing businessman's "for whatever it's worth" advice.

- A career is a game. First, you have to decide the game you want to play—is it engineering, sales, etc.? But keep it flexible. Our current CEO was an attorney, a product manager (working for me), our company treasurer, and then COO and president of a company subsidiary before becoming president and CEO of the parent company. In any game you must know the rules and the nuances—where you can stretch and experiment. You have to prepare well.

  > Richard recommends *When Character was King*, by Peggy Noonan

- Stretch. Take reasonable, informed risks. Know that there will be bumps and sometimes stumbles. Pick yourself up, dust yourself off, reflect, learn, and know that you are better for having endured.
- Believe it or not, common sense is really important.

- Every morning when I wake up, and this may be hard to believe, I think of the 18,000 Hormel Foods employees and families. I tell myself, "You have to do well, because these employees and their families are counting on you." Be responsible. You must want to be accountable.

- No matter what the job is, good communication is critical. Proper English (and Spanish, Chinese—more so every day) is so important—reading, writing, and speaking. In my group, we have a philosophy: "TNT" ("Talk Not Type"). The best way to get things done is to talk face to face. Shut off the computers, and stop sending e-mail after e-mail—many of which are typed simply to protect one's behind.

- Train your mind to think strategically. Have a very short list of strategies and communicate them well, often, and broadly. Create reasonable and measurable objectives, and hold people accountable. Establish critical paths, and have meetings once in a while to understand the progress. Trust your team to meet the objectives on time, but hold them accountable if they don't.

"You can learn more about a person in a moment of play than a lifetime of conversation."

- If your company does not encourage your ideas and input, leave.

- Get things done!!!

- I have a saying that I really believe in, so much that I do not remember if it is mine or if it came from someone else. It goes "You learn more about a person in a moment of play than in a lifetime of conversation."

- Another quote that I really like came from Senator Feargal Quinn, founder of the famous Superquinn supermarket chain in Ireland. In talking about marketing to bring customers into his stores he said, "If you want to catch fish, you must listen to the stream."

- One final statement (it came from package design firm Tad Ware & Company, which has been our partner for decades) is "Jump higher—worlds await. Getting there is all the fun." Tad Ware used a symbol of a leaping antelope along with it. To me it's not just an international marketing tagline; this has an expanded meaning. I can tell you, my kids grew tired of me quoting this to them. But I think it says so much, so simply. Stretch even though you may fumble, because there is so much opportunity—and enjoy the ride.

Jonathan Judge
President & CEO
PAYCHEX, INC.

- A career is a marathon—not a sprint. In the early part of your career, make sure you take the time to learn the fundamentals—both external and internal—about your company and chosen industry. If you try to take on responsibilities before you're ready, you'll probably not perform very well and you'll hurt your long-term prospects. The more you understand the details, the better—because throughout your career you'll be making decisions and judgments where correctness will be heavily influenced by your understanding of the basics.
- Be careful to never sacrifice long-term integrity for short-term gain—regardless of the size of the gain. When managers and executives are selected, one of the key criteria used to make that selection is the character and integrity of the candidate.
- If your career is important to you, don't abdicate the responsibility of your development to someone else. Of course, you

should take as much help as is offered, but ultimately, the person who should be responsible for building the strongest set of experiences and skills is you.

- The key difference between a manager and a non-manager is not the technical proficiency of the manager—it is the fact that the manager has the responsibility of the care and development of others, and the non-manager does not. Focus on your people, their needs, and the help they need to remove the obstacles to their success. Learn to get your personal satisfaction from the success of your subordinates—not your own.
- Being a good manager is not that hard. If you want to be a good manager, take out two pieces of blank paper. Then think about all the great managers you've had and write down on the first page all the things they did to make you feel that way. On the second page, do the same thing, only this time list all the attributes of the managers you really disliked. Now, do the things on page one, and don't do the things on page two!

Jay Horwitz
Vice President of Media Relations
NEW YORK METS

Don't be a clock-watcher, and never ever be late.

Also, words that never should be uttered are "He never called me back, and that is why I don't have the information." Always find a way to get the information.

Larry Levy
Chairman
LEVY RESTAURANTS

The following are a few hard-earned truths and quotations that have inspired me over the course of my career.

- "There are no failures, only expensive learning experiences."
- "Try to be one of those rare people who genuinely enjoy their career. You will probably enjoy life more and be better at what you do than anyone else."
- "Listen more than you speak. If God had wanted you to talk more than listen, he would have given you two mouths instead of two ears."
- "There is no such thing as a good deal with a bad partner."
- "Take your job seriously, but not yourself."
- "Catch people in the act of doing good things."

Last but not least is a quote from Daniel Burnham, the principal architect for the World's Columbian Exposition (Chicago World's Fair) in 1893. I enlarged it to three feet wide by six feet long, and it has been hanging in my office since 1976. I read it daily:

"Make no little plans. They have no magic to stir men's blood, and probably themselves will not be realized. Make big plans; aim high in hope and work, remembering that a noble, logical diagram once recorded will never die, but long after you are gone will be a living thing, asserting itself with ever-growing insistency. Remember that our sons and grandsons are going to do things

that would stagger us. Let your watchword be order and your beacon beauty."

Of course if Daniel were alive today, he would have amended one section to read "your sons and daughters and your grandsons and granddaughters." But they're words to live by nonetheless!

Steve Cushman
President
SANTA BARBARA REGION CHAMBER OF COMMERCE

These quotes are excerpts from poems that I have written.

1. Business is anything you can get away with.
2. Stumbling along always seems to lead to a new way home.
3. We drift through life trailing tentacles of remembrance.
4. I want to be judged by my dreams.
5. The older I get, the better I was.
6. Some mistakes are just too much fun not to repeat.
7. And of what are you made…That these thousands of shadows have crossed over you?
8. Through the fiercest storm, the darkest night…always a tiny patch of blue.
9. …and in all this…there are messages, indeed, inscrutable truths and meanings…about life, the universe and everything.

Frank Libutti, Lt. Gen., USMC (Retired)
Chairman & CEO
DIGITAL FUSION, INC.

Here are lessons learned over thirty-five years in the Marine Corps, a year and a half with NYPD, and nineteen months with the Department of Homeland Security:

- Be the coach more than the critic in mentoring your officers, particularly when working with young, company-grade officers (lieutenants and captains).
- As a new commander/boss, follow three simple rules:
    1. Know your war plans/missions thoroughly. Focus on your "readiness" factors.
    2. Know all aspects of your financial plans, current financial status, and budget process.
    3. Take all necessary actions during the conduct of your first field exercise/command to excel during post-exercise/major training events. This will immediately enhance your reputation and give you and your team instant credibility.
- I'm a big believer in the theme and philosophy of the book *Blink*, by Malcolm Gladwell: that a trained mind has the power to make good split-second decisions.
- I would suggest that young professionals review General Colin Powell's eighteen leadership lessons. Google "General Powell" and you will find them.
- As a senior officer, I used to tell the colonels and new generals that if there were one pill they should take in the morning,

it should be for wisdom...and if there were a second pill, it should be for humility.
- And finally, always take care of your troops/employees; they are the heart and soul of your team.

Sam O'Krent
President
O'KRENT'S ABBEY FLOORING CENTER

- There are two sides to every story.
- Take the time to listen to others.
- Never worry about your own pocket. As long as you are focused on your customer's pocket, yours will be full.
- Have fun!
- Surround yourself with heavyweights. You do not have to be the most knowledgeable as long as you have resources at your fingertips.
- It is not what you know, it is who you know.
- Don't be afraid to spend money—it's an investment.
- Change is always good. If you do today what you did yesterday, you will have tomorrow what you have today.
- There is no greater feeling than helping someone else. Always give back to your community.
- Network, network, network.

Bill Young
Chief Executive Officer
BILL YOUNG PRODUCTIONS

- Surround yourself with people who expect the best from you.
- Seek a job—and a career—that pushes you.
- Always give more than is expected.
- Learn to be a good listener.
- Find the best teachers…and listen to them.
- Give credit to others; they will fuel your success.
- Don't be too cool to say that you don't understand something. Ask questions until you do!
- Don't gossip. Say what you have to say only to the appropriate people.
- Don't become involved in office politics. Walk away instead.
- Always be honest—always!
- Build your career with integrity. Live your life with integrity.
- Always do what you say you will do.

Randall Fox
President
METALS USA

- Never say no to an opportunity, no matter how challenging and difficult it appears. You will learn more and distinguish yourself for taking on tough assignments. I have learned more from my failures in these tasks than I have ever learned from all of my triumphs.

- Marry the right person. Success in the workplace is extremely difficult if your home life is in turmoil. I credit the love and support of my wife as the greatest contribution to my success.
- Never, ever compromise your ethics and morals. Nothing can damage you more.
- Remember, the Lord will place you exactly where he wants you. It is your job to do something with the opportunities and people he places in your path.

QUESTIONS AND ANSWERS

*Leaders speak about their own young careers and
the young professionals of today.*

15

The leaders of today are concerned about the leaders of tomorrow, but they are also very excited about the young generation and what we bring to the workforce. These leaders of industry answered questions regarding their own young careers and their feelings about today's young professionals.

Joe Izganics

Former President, Southern Division
THE HOME DEPOT CORPORATION

When you started your career, did you know where you were headed? Did you plan or expect to be where you are today?

No. While we all have aspirations to excel in our jobs, I am not sure many of us know where we are planning to go or, more important, where we can go. I can say that by staying focused on the current prize, while setting immediate realistic goals and more lofty future goals, you can control your own destiny.

Were there any times or moments in the early part of your career that you remember as being defining?

The most defining moment in my career was accepting a high-level position outside of my area of expertise and immediate control. I may have worked harder than I ever had to in previous positions and at times felt I was in over my head. I persevered, however, and was very successful. The knowledge I gained helped me to further my career. The important learning was that I had to draw upon many resources and relationships I had developed through the years. The people you meet throughout your career can be invaluable resources. Be sure to take the time to stay connected and foster those relationships.

Which of your characteristics or traits do you feel helped you the most to achieve your goals?

Perseverance. We all need to realize that we will hit bumps in the road, and how you deal with them will determine how well you will do. If you treat bumps in the road and temporary setbacks as opportunities to improve your performance, you will learn valuable lessons that will help you in the future.

What did you do to continue learning, or what sort of professional development did you do in the early part of your career?

I have been fortunate to be able to participate in continuing retail education classes. While these are very helpful, my best learnings have come from spending time with associates throughout the company, and many times from those outside of my areas of responsibility. While education is important, drawing upon your own experiences and the experiences of others is far more important than any case studies.

Did you have any mentors, and how did you best utilize them?

I have had many mentors throughout the years. My best mentors have been people who have challenged me outside of my comfort zone. My advice is to stay connected with your mentors so that you continue to have valuable resources to call upon if needed.

Looking at young professionals today, what excites you the most?

Their eagerness to succeed.

What concerns you the most?

The perception that some roles are beneath them and the failure to realize the learnings that can be had from performing multiple jobs at different levels— that this can not only help them in their current positions, but can help them to succeed in achieving their goals. As I have stated earlier, we all will experience setbacks. A positive attitude to deal with them and overcome them is key to achieving your goals.

In looking back, what would you have done differently to prepare you for your current role?

While I was very open to accepting multiple roles throughout my career in my field, I was reluctant to accept roles outside of my field. While I was able to become well versed and successful, my career was slowed by not having more fully rounded experience.

Deirdre Connelly
President
NORTH AMERICAN PHARMACEUTICALS,
GLAXOSMITHKLINE

What did you do while in school to prepare yourself for the workforce?

My mom and dad had an insurance company in Puerto Rico. My dad was a great coach, and I had an opportunity to learn from and observe him. He let me go on field rides, and I got to set up meetings with his clients and friends. The exposure to customer interactions at an early age equipped me with skills for a future job.

When you started your career, did you know where you were headed? Did you plan or expect to be where you are today?

I did not plan to be the president of North American Pharmaceuticals for GlaxoSmithKline, nor the president of Lilly USA previously, but it never occurred to me that I could not do such a thing. However, I did know I wanted to be in the pharmaceutical industry. I was really interested in being able to work in marketing, while at the same time helping people and doing good for society. There were no opportunities in marketing when I began with Lilly, so I took a job in sales. I loved it! Being able to interact with our customers was significant to my understanding of our business. I also worked with great sales professionals and saw so many great opportunities within the company. I believe that anybody with passion and drive can do whatever they put their mind to.

Do you remember making a large mistake in the early part of your career, and what came from it?

I made quite a few mistakes. We usually think we know more than we actually do. My main mistake came from thinking I knew how to lead and manage before I actually did. I needed to stop telling people things and start listening to them. I needed to be more of a coach rather than a policeman.

Which of your characteristics or traits do you feel helped you the most to achieve your goals?

Probably that I have been a dedicated student, and I have an eagerness to constantly learn about management, leadership, and myself. I embraced opportunities to learn from my peers and leadership within the company.

Were there any times or moments in the early part of your career that you remember as being defining?

It was not just one time in the early part of my career that was defining, but maybe an entire approach. I had a mind-set of creating opportunities for myself and the company. I looked for ways to change the job for the better. I would present different marketing and sales tactics to my teammates and suggest ways to improve processes. I loved coming up with creative and fresh ways to do things. I think young professionals can differentiate themselves from others just by looking for and acting on opportunities to improve their job and organization.

What did you do to continue learning, or what sort of professional development did you do in the early part of your career?

As I mentioned, I embraced learning and especially reading. Reading has been integral to my personal growth. I can't say that I am a big reader of today's more popular business books, because I prefer biographies of older leaders, such as Abraham Lincoln. Books on leadership today have not seen the test of time just yet. But people like Abraham Lincoln—their leadership traits and skills have definitely passed the test of time.

Looking at young professionals today, what excites you the most?

I like that young professionals speak their mind. Their work/life balance is great and is definitely a priority for them. I admire our younger generation's concern for those other than themselves.

What concerns you the most?

Their sense of commitment is not as strong as that of previous generations. I have noticed a sense of pride and entitlement that sometimes gets in the way of their discipline and willingness to work hard. My main concern is that young professionals hold less ownership for themselves. Parents calling college professors is an alarming reality. This is partially the parents' fault for continuing to hover over their children, but the students themselves need to be more independent and hold themselves accountable for their actions.

Craig Milan
President
ROYAL CELEBRITY TOURS

What advice do you give young professionals starting their careers?

The nineteenth century was England's. The twentieth century was generally centered around America and was when America rose to great power. The twenty-first century is going to be China's. As such, almost every large company either has a China strategy or is working on one. Whether you are in manufacturing or the service sector, China presents a huge opportunity with its enormous population base and growing affluence.

My advice to anyone in college now is to become an expert on China.

Learn the language (Mandarin), study the culture, and learn how to do business there. Whilst the Chinese have a Communist political system, they are in fact very much capitalists and are focused on economic growth and wealth creation. American students who graduate from college or a university with skill sets related to doing business in China will be very attractive to many corporations.

I believe that graduates with these skill sets will be the ones best positioned to land interesting and well-paying jobs at major companies. They will also be in a position of visibility as companies are scrambling to find individuals who have knowledge of and/or experience in China.

David Chard, PhD
Dean of the Annette Caldwell Simmons School of Education
& Human Development
SOUTHERN METHODIST UNIVERSITY

What is your educational background? What did you do while in school to prepare yourself for the workforce?

I attended a small public school in eastern Michigan. I then attended a mid-sized public four-year university and prepared to teach mathematics and chemistry at the high school level. I was fortunate to have strong preparation in cognitive-behavioral principles and strong disciplinary development. After teaching for a number of years, I returned to a large research university to pursue my PhD in special education. In all cases, my studies were coupled with exceptional practical experiences that prepared me to step into leadership roles in education rather quickly. These included student teaching, supervision of new teachers, and opportunities to assist on large-scale educational research projects.

When you started your career, did you know where you were headed? Did you plan or expect to be where you are today?

No. I have to be honest, I did not always know what I wanted to be. Consequently, I found myself trying things that just seemed to make sense. I liked working in schools, so trying to be a teacher made sense. I enjoyed mathematics and science, so it made sense to pursue that avenue. After teaching, I realized that I was always working with students who struggled academically. It made sense for me to pursue a PhD in special education, an area that is perennially underserved and for which research was valued and promoted.

Were there any times or moments in the early part of your career that you remember as being defining?

Of course, my experience as a U.S. Peace Corps volunteer in southern Africa was particularly defining. I worked in a village school for two years and frequently would travel to the even smaller villages that were my students' homes. I recognized then that for many high school students in that region, very little was done in the early grades to help students excel in the higher grades. So in my third year, I developed a program that involved going to small villages on horseback to work with elementary school teachers who worked with the students before they moved to high school. In many cases, these teachers were teaching multiple grades, and they had few resources and very little professional development. I tried to provide all these to them during my brief visits. This theme of working to prevent difficulties early in children's educational careers became a theme in my graduate work, as has professional development for teachers. The program I had developed became a model for the Peace Corps in sub-Saharan Africa.

Did you have any mentors, and how did you best use them?

I have always sought out mentors. In all stages of my life, I have had exceptional models who were great at coaching me through difficult decisions and periods. A cousin who was an exceptional mentor helped me understand how the best teachers work with students. In the Peace Corps, I worked with two veteran educators who both helped me improve my own teaching, but also encouraged me to become a leader in education. I was able to benefit from watching them work with teachers and children, and they taught me the importance of education that focuses on student outcomes. As a professor and now as a dean, I have mentors who help me with all aspects of my career, from scholarship to operational decisions. I am careful to seek mentorship from individuals who excel at what they do. This sometimes involves crossing traditional academic and nonacademic barriers to look for advice and guidance from unlikely sources.

Did you ever make a large mistake as a young professional—and if so, what did you learn from it?

I am a very cautious person and haven't made any significant mistakes. The decisions I have made about career moves that didn't turn out to be the best were ultimately great ways to learn lessons. However, in all cases, I have no regrets.

Which of your characteristics or traits do you feel helped you the most to achieve your goals?

I am a very good listener. This translates into my being able to collect lots of information about people, to observe their behaviors and habits, to understand their needs, and then to make useful decisions about how to solve problems. I am also very eager to help people understand how to improve things for themselves. I am intensely interested in how people's histories, experiences, culture, and values affect their decisions, and I work tirelessly to try to bring these areas together in my work to improve schools for all children.

Looking at young professionals today, what excites you the most?

I am most excited about the degree of commitment of young professionals today—the desire to do more than make their fortune. There is a robust energy in today's young professionals; they wish to take their skills and knowledge and to give back to society. This is something that, as a former Peace Corps volunteer, I find very exciting. Today, however, we see this sort of spirit in more than just the small segment of society that, historically, felt they needed to give back to their communities and the world. Today, many young professionals see it as an important part of who they are.

What concerns you the most?

I believe that many young professionals are at the front edge of a very transformative time in our history. The baby-boom generation is slowly moving out, and young professionals must fill the gap in leadership across professions. These individuals may not be prepared to take on the high degree of responsibility that will be expected, because the previous generation has been in the leadership position for so long. Moreover, in the most critical professions, including education, I believe that many young professionals do not see a long-term commitment, because we have not provided sufficient incentives for them to work in the human service areas.

In looking back, what would you have done differently to prepare you for your current role?

I had no intention of becoming an administrator in higher education. I believe it would have been helpful to have a stronger focus on management in my past. However, I have learned a great deal on the job and feel I am a strong supporter of the individuals who make up my staff and faculty.

Frank Felicella
Former Chairman & CEO
BUILDER'S SQUARE

What is your educational background? What did you do while in school to prepare yourself for the workforce?

I received a Bachelor of Science in business administration. I took all the normal business courses at Quinnipiac University, which included four years of accounting. I also had a very unusual elective balance in the sciences, with physiology and sociology, which allowed me to earn a BS instead of a BA. This was a conscious decision I made to learn more about managing and leading people. I worked all throughout my five years in school to pay for my education, the final two years at Sears, Roebuck and Co. While at school, I rose to the level of checklist executive and was running customer service, delivery service, and repair service.

When you started your career, did you know where you were headed? Did you plan or expect to be where you are today?

I approached graduation looking for a job. Recruiters on my campus were the U.S. government (IRS, CIA, FBI), oil companies, and financial companies that were looking for accounting majors. My early goals were financial goals— $1,000 multiplied by my age. My store manager talked me into interviewing with Sears. At the time, store managers for Sears made more than the president of the United States and retired early with profit sharing. I was offered a store trainee position in their next class in Hicksville, Long Island, New York.

I always worked as if my current job would be my last job, and I continued to get promoted every nine to eighteen months. I then moved on from Sears and held executive positions with E. J. Korvette, Collins & Aikman, Target, Handy Dan, and Dayton-Hudson.

I eventually landed the dream job of president and CEO of Builder's Square. The challenge was to fix it and/or sell it. We fixed it and then we sold it. The new owners were told if they moved headquarters, the management team would resign. They moved and we all resigned. That was the first time I retired. But then I continued doing what I was good at—fixing bad companies. After accomplishments like saving the Texas Open, a PGA Tour event, and turning Apollo Gate Operators around and selling it, I finally have retired once again. As you can see, I went where the work took me by picking the best jobs of those that were offered. By staying focused on my current job at hand, I was never short of opportunities to advance and get to where I did.

Were there any times or moments in the early part of your career that you remember as being defining?

I made the decision to leave "mother Sears" when we were told we would sit in a position for twenty-four to thirty-six months without promotion. It was considered a big gamble, because it was said that companies would hire us, suck us dry of Sears information, then fire us. Those who left Sears were the boldest of the management, and not all of us met with success.

What sort of professional development did you do in the early part of your career?

I took every job offered to me. I was the biggest complainer in Sears that systems were being written by programmers and not merchants. I complained so much, the "powers that be" made me systems co-coordinator. Hell, I could not even spell "computer," let alone lead a group to fix what was wrong. I surrounded myself with the best people I could beg, borrow, or steal. We fixed the issues and came up with many good ideas. This experience of leading technical people and learning the power of the computer helped my career wherever I went.

Did you have any mentors, and how did you best use them?

The list is long and distinguished, because I always took all the time I could to ask questions and get sponsors. Store managers, vice presidents, presidents, CEOs, and teachers—names you would recognize, like Kenneth Macke, CEO of Target; Bill Greehey, CEO of Valero; author Ken Blanchard; Ernesto Ancira, CEO of Ancira Enterprises; astronaut Neil Armstrong; and too many others to mention. I tried to take only the best from all these people and others and to incorporate them into my plans and my management style. I am still learning today.

Looking at young professionals today, what excites you the most?

The blank slate they all come with and the changes they are about to live.

What concerns you the most?

The fact that the education system has created mediocrity. The ability to think and speak on your feet or on the run is not present in most young professionals. The mentality is that they are entitled to something because they completed higher education.

Did you ever make a large mistake as a young professional—and if so, what did you learn from it?

I made many mistakes, but one still sticks in my mind. I was a young department manager on my second assignment buying and selling men's shirts and accessories. I made an aggressive sales plan and overbought. My merchandise managers and store managers let me run with it. I ended the season with almost as much as I sold. The managers told me to figure out a way to get the inventory back in line. I did so by selling excess inventory to other stores for a sales promotion I thought up. The lesson was, if you get into a mess, you need to clean it up.

In looking back, what would you have done differently to prepare you for your most recent roles?

I refuse to look back and say, "What if...?" In fact, I am still looking forward to see what could be. Take the opportunities that come to you, because you can never go back and start over. Learn from each job, whether you like it or not. Treat every job as if it were your last job.

BE EXTRAORDINARY!
Take advantage of mediocrity, and seize the opportunity!

In all my business dealings and interactions, I am always amazed at the acceptance of mediocrity. The great business book *Good to Great*, by Jim Collins, lays out the differences between "good" and "great," and remarks that most people settle for being good instead of striving to be great. I'll take it one step further, however: I feel that most people settle for mediocrity, and miss out on being either good or great.

Every young professional has an incredible opportunity to differentiate himself or herself from peers and coworkers. My fervent hope is that in reading this book, young professionals who have the desire and the drive to succeed "by any means necessary" will find out that, in fact, they have those very means within their power. And that the journey to success can be easier, less ruthless, and more energizing than they ever imagined.

It is unrealistic to believe that you will adopt every suggestion in this book and immediately act upon it. However, if you can introduce a few concepts—such as pre-call planning, challenging the norm, building your network, or whatever you find to be most valuable—then you will certainly begin improving your career and differentiating yourself from the paycheck players.

In the past, every time I read a business or leadership book, I thought to myself, "If I do what this book suggests, then I won't stand out, because everyone else who read the book will be doing it." But the truth is, not everyone who reads this book (or any other book) will actually do what is recommended. Most professionals could write down a list of things they know they could do to improve their career or jobs; however, the majority of people do not take action on all of these things. As Jonathan Judge said, there are plenty of paycheck players, and corporations know this and expect it. This is why there is a huge opportunity for those of you who are truly committed and passionate to make an impact on your career or workplace.

I recently attended a speaking event that featured Norm Brodsky and Bo Burlingham, authors of *The Knack*. While Norm was speaking of his businesses successes and failures, he smiled, pointed at himself, and said, "I am a smart man." When he paused, I looked around, thinking that it was a very weird thing to say. And then he continued: "But I don't want you to be smart like me, I want you to be wise. Because smart men learn from their mistakes, but wise men learn from the mistakes of others." I cannot think of a more appropriate theme for this entire book.

Through the mistakes, lessons, and experiences of industry and community leaders included in this book, I hope you will see the tremendous opportunity you have to be extraordinary in your career. Be wise, not smart. Continually look for ways to Soak It Up, and then remember to Jump In! Success in your career will surely follow.